S.No	CHAPTERS	PAGE

Introduction: Understanding Chrome Extensions

In today's digital world, web browsers are like your trusty tour guides through the vast landscape of the internet. They are the virtual vehicles that whisk you away to the world of information, connect you with friends and family, open doors to online shopping, and provide endless avenues for entertainment. Picture them as your loyal companions on your digital journey.

But here's where the magic happens: browsers like Chrome can do even more with a little bit of extra help. This help comes in the form of "Chrome extensions." Think of them as tiny tools or helpers that you can add to your browser. These little wonders can make your browser supercharged, like giving your trusty companion some incredible superpowers. They can change how websites look, add cool features, and make your online life smoother and more enjoyable.

In this chapter, we're going to dive into the world of Chrome extensions. We'll take a close look at what they are, why they're so fascinating, and how they can take your online adventures to the next level.

Now, you might be wondering why we're focusing on Chrome. Well, it's because Chrome is like the superhero among browsers. It's not just popular; it's also an excellent place to discover and use these extensions. Chrome offers a vast playground for your digital adventures, and we're here to be your guides.

So, get ready to step into the fascinating universe of Chrome extensions. It's a world where your browser becomes a versatile tool for incredible online experiences.

What Are Browser Extensions?

Imagine you're customizing your car. You can add cool gadgets like a GPS, a music player, or even a cup holder. These extras make your car more functional and fun. Well, think of browser extensions as those cool gadgets, but for your web browser.

At its core, a browser extension is like a small, helpful program that you can add to your web browser. It's like giving your browser a superpower or a handy tool. These extensions can change how websites look, add new features, or make tasks on the web much easier.

For instance, imagine you're browsing an online store, and you want to compare prices easily. An extension could pop up and show you the best deals right there on the page. Or, when you're reading news online, an extension might help you highlight and save important information. It's like having a virtual assistant that knows exactly what you need when you need it.

Now, let's talk about why they're called "extensions." Think of them as the magic wand for your browser that turns it from a basic tool into a Swiss Army knife of the digital world. They extend your browser's capabilities, making it a versatile companion for all your online adventures.

Why Chrome Extensions Matter

You might be wondering, "Why focus on Chrome extensions?" Well, here's why they matter:

Think of your web browser as a superhero. It already does an amazing job of taking you anywhere on the internet. But even superheroes have sidekicks and special gadgets, right? That's where Chrome extensions come in. They're like the trusty sidekicks of your web browser, here to enhance your online experience.

1. **Customization**: Chrome extensions are like personalized tools for your browser. They let you tailor your online experience. Whether you want to boost productivity, enhance security, or simply have more fun, there's a Chrome extension for you. It's like wearing your favorite online superhero costume. Extensions make your browser uniquely yours.

2. **Enhanced Functionality**: Chrome extensions are like magical add-ons. They can give your browser new superpowers. Need to block annoying ads, manage passwords securely, or supercharge your online shopping? Chrome extensions have you covered. They transform your browser into a high-tech tool, ready to handle any online challenge

   Think of it this way: Your browser is like a sleek sports car. It's fast, efficient, and gets you where you want to go. But with Chrome extensions, it's like turbocharging that sports car, adding wings and rockets. Now, your browser can not only navigate the digital highway but also soar through it.

These extensions are like the Swiss Army knife of your browser, equipped with tools for every situation. They're your digital companions, always ready to assist and enhance your online adventures.

But why Chrome specifically? Well, Google's Chrome browser is like the superhero base camp for extensions. It's the place where developers create these amazing tools to help you. It's like the bustling city where all the superheroes gather to prepare for their missions.

So, as we delve deeper into the world of Chrome extensions, remember that you're stepping into a realm where your browser becomes a dynamic and versatile tool, thanks to these incredible add-ons.

Types of Chrome Extensions

Chrome extensions come in a delightful variety, much like the flavors at an ice cream parlor. Each type serves a unique purpose, adding a sprinkle of functionality or a dash of fun to your browsing experience:

1. **Productivity Extensions**: Picture these as your digital assistants. They streamline your work, manage your tasks, and keep you organized. It's like having a virtual secretary, always ready to help you tackle your to-do list.

2. **Security Extensions**: Think of these as your online bodyguards. They shield you from scams, viruses, and prying eyes, ensuring your online world stays secure. It's like having a vigilant guardian that makes your online adventures worry-free.

3. **Entertainment Extensions**: Ever wanted to add a dash of fun to your browser? Entertainment extensions are your go-to choice. They infuse playfulness into your browsing with themes, games, and creative tools. It's

like transforming your browser into a playground, where fun is just a click away.

4. **Development Tools**: If you're a web developer or enthusiast, these are your trusty toolbox. Development extensions are like a treasure trove for those who craft the web. They offer a suite of features for web development, debugging, and testing. Need to inspect the structure of a web page, debug JavaScript code, or analyze network activity? Development extensions make it a breeze. They're like having a team of skilled developers at your side, helping you build, optimize, and enhance websites. It's the key to unlocking the full potential of web technology, turning your browser into a developer's paradise.

With these diverse extensions, there's something for everyone, catering to your unique online preferences. It's like having a buffet of options for your digital journey, where you can select the perfect flavor for each online adventure.

5. **Accessibility Extensions**: These extensions are champions of inclusivity. They make the web more accessible to people with disabilities. Whether it's screen readers, text-to-speech, or magnification, accessibility extensions ensure that everyone can navigate and enjoy the online world comfortably.

6. **Shopping and Price Comparison Extensions**: Savvy shoppers rejoice! These extensions are your bargain-hunting companions. They automatically find and apply coupons, track prices, and compare deals while you

shop online. It's like having a personal shopper who always finds the best discounts.

7. **Note-Taking and Research Extensions**: For students, researchers, or anyone who loves learning, these extensions are invaluable. They simplify note-taking, citation management, and research organization. It's like having a virtual library at your fingertips, helping you gather and organize information effortlessly.

8. **Social Media Extensions**: These extensions are for the social butterflies. They enhance your social media experience with features like post scheduling, analytics, and content sharing. It's like having a social media manager right in your browser.

With such a diverse array of extensions, Chrome becomes a versatile tool, adapting to your specific needs and preferences. It's like having a digital Swiss Army knife, ready to tackle any online task or adventure.

9. **Language and Translation Extensions**: These are your language tutors, making the world more accessible. They help you translate text, learn new languages, and improve your language skills. It's like having a personal language coach right in your browser, breaking down language barriers and opening doors to global communication. These extensions are not just tools; they are bridges between cultures and knowledge.

10. **Privacy and Ad-Blocking Extensions**: Concerned about your online privacy? These extensions are your digital shields, guarding your virtual realm. They block trackers, ads, and keep your personal information safe from

prying eyes. It's like having an invisible cloak for your online identity, ensuring your digital presence remains private and secure. With these extensions, your online activities become your own, away from unwanted surveillance.

11. **News and RSS Feed Extensions**: Stay updated effortlessly with these extensions that bring the latest news and articles directly to your browser. It's like having a custom newsstand that caters to your interests, keeping you informed about the topics that matter most. These extensions transform your browser into a portal of knowledge, delivering information right to your fingertips.

12. **Task and Project Management Extensions**: If you're juggling tasks and projects, these extensions are your organizers. They help you plan, track progress, and collaborate effectively. It's like having a project manager to keep everything on track, ensuring your work and personal projects run smoothly. These extensions empower you to be more efficient, turning your browser into a productivity powerhouse.

With this diverse array of extensions, Chrome becomes your ultimate digital companion, adapting to your unique needs and interests.

Why Chrome Extensions Are Irreplaceable

Chrome extensions aren't just handy add-ons; they are the lifeblood of your browser, elevating your online experience to new heights. Here's why they are truly irreplaceable:

1. **Tailored Experience**: Extensions allow you to tailor your browser to your exact needs. It's like having a personalized internet experience, where your browser understands your preferences and adapts accordingly. Imagine browsing the web with a tool that knows what you love and delivers it effortlessly. That's the power of Chrome extensions.

2. **Efficiency Boost**: Whether it's streamlining tasks, enhancing security, or adding entertainment, extensions supercharge your online efficiency. They're like the turbo boosters that propel you forward in the digital world, making every online action smoother and faster. With extensions, you become a digital superhero, accomplishing tasks with ease.

3. **Endless Possibilities**: With thousands of extensions available, the possibilities are boundless. Whatever you can imagine, there's likely an extension for it. It's like having a universe of digital tools at your disposal, ready to make your online dreams a reality. From creative design to data analysis, extensions are your versatile companions.

4. **Constant Evolution**: Chrome extensions are continually evolving. Developers create new ones to address emerging needs, ensuring your browser remains at the forefront of web technology. It's like having a browser that never gets old, always adapting to the latest trends and technologies. With extensions, your browser is a living, breathing entity, constantly improving.

   In summary, Chrome extensions are the secret sauce that makes your browser not just a tool but a personalized, efficient, and ever-evolving companion in your online adventures. They transform your digital journey into an extraordinary experience, where every click is a step toward a more tailored and efficient online world.

How to Discover and Install Chrome Extensions

Now that you understand the incredible value of Chrome extensions, let's delve into how to discover and install them.

1. **Visit the Chrome Web Store**: The Chrome Web Store is your gateway to a treasure trove of extensions. Open Google Chrome, click on the three dots in the top-right corner, and select "Extensions." Then, click on "Open Chrome Web Store." Here, you can explore extensions by category, popularity, or search for specific ones.

2. **Browse and Search**: Explore the categories or use the search bar to find extensions that align with your needs. Whether it's productivity, security, or entertainment, you'll find a wide array of options.

3. **Read Reviews and Descriptions**: Before installing, it's wise to read user reviews and extension descriptions. This helps you gauge an extension's quality and functionality. Look for highly-rated extensions with positive feedback.

4. **Click "Add to Chrome"**: When you've found an extension you like, click on "Add to Chrome." A pop-up window will appear, asking for confirmation. Click "Add

Extension." The extension will be downloaded and installed.

5. **Explore Your New Tool**: After installation, you'll usually see the extension's icon in the top-right corner of your browser. Click on it to access its features and settings. Some extensions may require you to sign in or configure settings to unleash their full potential.

Now, armed with your newfound knowledge of Chrome extensions, you're ready to transform your browsing experience. Explore, discover, and enhance your online world with these powerful digital companions.

Managing and Organizing Your Chrome Extensions

Now that you've installed a few Chrome extensions, it's essential to keep them organized and manage them effectively. Here's how:

1. **Access the Extension Menu**: Click on the puzzle piece icon in the top-right corner of your browser. This icon represents your extensions. It's a hub where you can access, enable, or disable your installed extensions.

2. **Organize Your Extensions**: You can rearrange the order of your extensions by clicking and dragging their icons in the extension menu. This helps you prioritize and access your most frequently used extensions quickly.

3. **Enable and Disable**: If you want to temporarily disable an extension, click on its icon in the extension menu, and then toggle the switch to "off." This is handy if you

don't need an extension's functionality for a specific browsing session.

4. **Remove Unnecessary Extensions**: To remove an extension entirely, right-click on its icon in the extension menu and select "Remove from Chrome." This keeps your browser clutter-free and ensures you only have the extensions you truly need.

5. **Configure Extension Settings**: Some extensions have settings that you can customize. Right-click on the extension's icon and choose "Options" or "Settings" to access these configurations. Tailor the extension to your preferences.

6. **Stay Updated**: Keep your extensions up-to-date. Chrome automatically updates them, but it's good practice to check for updates manually by going to the Chrome menu > Extensions > Update.

By managing your Chrome extensions effectively, you ensure that they enhance your browsing experience without overwhelming your browser. With these tools at your disposal and your organizational skills, your online world becomes a well-tailored and efficient digital playground.

Managing and Organizing Your Chrome Extensions

Now that you've installed a few Chrome extensions, it's essential to keep them organized and manage them effectively. Here's how:

1. **Access the Extension Menu**: Click on the puzzle piece icon in the top-right corner of your browser. This icon represents your extensions. It's a hub where you can access, enable, or disable your installed extensions.

2. **Organize Your Extensions**: You can rearrange the order of your extensions by clicking and dragging their icons in the extension menu. This helps you prioritize and access your most frequently used extensions quickly.

3. **Enable and Disable**: If you want to temporarily disable an extension, click on its icon in the extension menu, and then toggle the switch to "off." This is handy if you don't need an extension's functionality for a specific browsing session.

4. **Remove Unnecessary Extensions**: To remove an extension entirely, right-click on its icon in the extension menu and select "Remove from Chrome." This keeps your browser clutter-free and ensures you only have the extensions you truly need.

5. **Configure Extension Settings**: Some extensions have settings that you can customize. Right-click on the extension's icon and choose "Options" or "Settings" to access these configurations. Tailor the extension to your preferences.

6. **Stay Updated**: Keep your extensions up-to-date. Chrome automatically updates them, but it's good practice to check for updates manually by going to the Chrome menu > Extensions > Update.

   By managing your Chrome extensions effectively, you ensure that they enhance your browsing experience without overwhelming your browser. With these tools at your disposal and your organizational skills, your online world becomes a well-tailored and efficient digital playground.

Chrome Extensions for Enhanced Productivity

Let's delve into how Chrome extensions can supercharge your productivity. In today's fast-paced digital world, time is precious, and these extensions can help you make the most of it:

1. **Todoist**: If you're a fan of to-do lists, Todoist is your best friend. It lets you organize tasks, set deadlines, and even collaborate with others. It's like having a personal assistant keeping track of your daily goals.

2. **LastPass**: Struggling to remember passwords? LastPass securely stores your login information and auto-fills it when needed. It's like having a digital keyring that unlocks the web effortlessly.

3. **StayFocusd**: Are distractions a constant hurdle? StayFocusd lets you set time limits on distracting websites, helping you stay focused on your work. It's like having a virtual workspace where distractions are minimized.

4. **Grammarly**: For impeccable writing, Grammarly checks your spelling and grammar as you type in emails, documents, or online forms. It's like having a grammar coach at your side, ensuring your words are always on point.

5. **Dark Reader**: If you work late or prefer dark-themed interfaces, Dark Reader turns bright web pages into soothing dark mode, reducing eye strain. It's like having a cozy reading nook on the web.

6. **Momentum**: Start your day right with Momentum. It replaces your new tab page with a serene dashboard featuring a to-do list, inspiring quotes, and a focus mode. It's like having a morning routine for your online world.

With these productivity-enhancing Chrome extensions, you can transform your browser into a productivity powerhouse. They save you time, keep you organized, and help you maintain focus. Whether you're tackling work projects, studying, or simply managing your daily life, these extensions are your trusted allies in the pursuit of efficiency.

Chapter 1: Getting Started with Chrome Extensions

Welcome to the exciting world of Chrome extension development! In this chapter, we'll embark on your journey to create powerful browser extensions that enhance your online experience and cater to your unique needs. Whether you're a seasoned developer or a curious beginner, we'll take you through the essential steps to get started.

Installing Chrome Developer Tools

Before diving into extension development, it's crucial to have the right tools at your disposal. Chrome Developer Tools is your Swiss Army knife for web development and extension creation. Here's how to set it up:

1. **Open Google Chrome**: Ensure you have Google Chrome installed on your computer. If not, download and install it from chrome.com.

2. **Access Developer Tools**: Open a new browser window, navigate to any webpage, and right-click anywhere on the page. Select "Inspect" or press **Ctrl+Shift+I**

(Windows/Linux) or **Cmd+Option+I** (Mac) to open Chrome's Developer Tools panel.

3. **Getting Familiar**: Take some time to explore the Developer Tools panel. You'll find a plethora of tools for debugging, inspecting elements, and more. Familiarize yourself with its layout and functionalities; it will be your trusted companion throughout this journey.

Choosing a Code Editor

A code editor is where the magic happens. It's the canvas for crafting your Chrome extensions. While there are numerous code editors available, you can choose one that suits your preferences. Here are a few popular options:

1. **Visual Studio Code**: A free, open-source editor with a robust extension ecosystem. It's lightweight, highly customizable, and supports various programming languages.

2. **Sublime Text**: Known for its speed and simplicity, Sublime Text is a favorite among developers. It offers powerful features like multiple selections and a distraction-free mode.

3. **Atom**: Developed by GitHub, Atom is a hackable text editor designed for the 21st century. It's highly customizable through packages and themes.

4. **Notepad++**: A Windows-based editor that's fast and efficient. It supports various languages and offers a user-friendly interface.

Choose the code editor that resonates with you, and let's move on to creating your first extension project.

Creating Your First Extension Project

Creating a Chrome extension project is akin to setting up your workspace. Here's a simplified step-by-step guide to initiate your journey:

1. **Create a Project Folder**: Start by creating a dedicated folder for your extension project. This folder will house all your extension files.

2. **Manifest File**: Every Chrome extension begins with a manifest file. This file provides essential information about your extension, including its name, version, permissions, and more. Create a file named **manifest.json** within your project folder.

3. **Define the Manifest**: Open the **manifest.json** file in your code editor and define the basic structure. At a minimum, include the extension's name and version.

```json
{
  "manifest_version": 3,
  "name": "My First Extension",
  "version": "1.0"
}
```

4. **Load Your Extension**: To load your extension into Chrome for testing, follow these steps:

   - Open Google Chrome.

- Go to **chrome://extensions/** or click on the three dots in the top-right corner, then select "Extensions."

- Enable "Developer mode" by toggling the switch.

- Click on "Load unpacked" and select your project folder. Your extension should now appear in the list of installed extensions.

Understanding Manifest Files

The **manifest.json** file is the blueprint of your extension. It defines important details like its name, version, description, permissions, and more. Here are some key components you should be aware of:

- **"name"**: This is the name of your extension that users will see.

- **"version"**: The version number of your extension.

- **"description"**: A brief description of what your extension does.

- **"permissions"**: Permissions are essential for your extension to interact with specific websites or features.

- **"background"**: This specifies a background script that can run in the background and perform tasks like handling events and managing data.

- **"content_scripts"**: Content scripts allow you to interact with the content of web pages.

Choosing a Code Editor

Choosing the right code editor is crucial for productive development. Consider your preferences and the features that matter most to you:

1. **Visual Studio Code (VS Code)**: VS Code is a versatile and highly extensible code editor. It offers a wide range of extensions to enhance your development workflow.

2. **Sublime Text**: Known for its speed and simplicity, Sublime Text is a lightweight code editor with a vibrant community of users and developers.

3. **Atom**: Atom, developed by GitHub, is a customizable and open-source code editor. It's known for its user-friendly interface and community-driven packages.

4. **Notepad++**: If you prefer a straightforward Windows-based code editor, Notepad++ is a fast and efficient choice.

You can start with any of these editors, and later chapters will cover specific extensions and tools to enhance your development experience.

Creating Your First Extension Project

Now that you're equipped with the necessary tools and a code editor, let's dive into creating your first Chrome extension project:

1. **Create a Project Folder**: Begin by creating a dedicated folder for your extension project. This folder will house all your extension files and assets.

2. **Manifest File**: Every Chrome extension starts with a manifest file. This file provides essential information about your extension, including its name, version,

permissions, and more. Create a new file named **manifest.jso**

```json
{
  "manifest_version": 3,
  "name": "My First Extension",
  "version": "1.0",
  "description": "An introduction to creating Chrome extensions",
  "permissions": [
    "activeTab"
  ],
  "action": {
    "default_popup": "popup.html",
    "default_icon": {
      "16": "images/icon16.png",
      "48": "images/icon48.png",
      "128": "images/icon128.png"
    }
  }
}
```

n within your project folder.

In this example, we've defined the name, version, description, and permissions for our extension. We've also specified a popup HTML file and icons of various sizes.

3. **Create HTML and JavaScript Files**: For this basic example, we'll need an HTML file (**popup.html**) and a JavaScript file (**popup.js**). These files will form the core of our extension's functionality.

4. **Load Your Extension**: To test your extension locally, follow these steps:

   • Open Google Chrome.

- Go to **chrome://extensions/** or click on the three dots in the top-right corner, then select "Extensions."

- Enable "Developer mode" by toggling the switch.

- Click on "Load unpacked" and select your project folder. Your extension should now appear in the list of installed extensions.

With these initial steps, you've set up your development environment, created the foundation for your Chrome extension, and are ready to delve deeper into extension components, HTML, CSS, JavaScript, and user interface design. Get ready to bring your extension to life!

Chapter 2: HTML, CSS, and JavaScript Basics

HTML Essentials for Extensions

HTML, or HyperText Markup Language, is the foundation of web content, including Chrome extensions. In this section, we will explore the essentials of HTML, gaining a deeper understanding of its elements, structure, and best practices.

Introduction to HTML

At its core, HTML is a markup language used to structure content on the web. It is composed of elements, each enclosed in tags, that define the content's meaning and structure. These elements provide the building blocks for web pages and Chrome extension interfaces.

HTML Elements

HTML offers a rich set of elements, each serving a specific purpose. Here are some fundamental HTML elements:

1. **Headings (<h1> to <h6>)**: Headings are used to define the hierarchical structure of a page, with **<h1>** being the highest level and **<h6>** the lowest.

2. **Paragraphs (<p>)**: Paragraph elements encapsulate text content, creating readable blocks of text.

3. **Links (<a>)**: The anchor element is used for creating hyperlinks to other web pages or resources.

4. **Images (<img>)**: Image elements embed images within a web page or extension interface.

5. **Lists (<ul>, <ol>, <li>)**: Lists come in two forms: unordered (**<ul>**) and ordered (**<ol>**), with list items (**<li>**) defining individual list entries.

6. **Forms (<form>, <input>, <button>)**: Forms allow users to input data and submit it. Elements like text inputs, radio buttons, and submit buttons are commonly used.

Syntax

HTML relies on a straightforward syntax that consists of opening and closing tags. Tags are enclosed in angle brackets, with the closing tag preceded by a forward slash. For example:

```html
<p>This is a paragraph.</p>
<a href="https://www.example.com">Visit Example</a>
```

In this example, **<p>** encloses a paragraph, while **<a>** defines a hyperlink with the **href** attribute specifying the link's destination.

Creating the HTML Structure for Extensions

In the context of Chrome extensions, HTML is instrumental in crafting user interfaces for various components, such as popup windows, options pages, and content scripts. Here's how HTML structure is typically used:

Popup HTML

Popup pages are displayed when users click on the extension's icon. These pages often contain concise information or quick actions. To create a basic popup interface, we use HTML elements to structure the content and CSS to style it.

Options Page

Chrome extensions commonly include options that users can configure to personalize their experience. Options pages are created using HTML forms, allowing users to input their preferences and save settings.

Best Practices for Writing Clean HTML Code

Maintaining clean and well-structured HTML code is crucial for the readability, maintainability, and accessibility of your extension. Consider the following best practices:

Indentation and Formatting

Consistent indentation and formatting make your code more accessible and understandable. Proper indentation ensures that nested elements are clearly visible, making your code easier to navigate.

```html
<div>
    <p>This is properly indented.</p>
</div>
```

Semantic HTML

Semantic HTML elements, such as **<header>**, **<nav>**, and **<footer>**, enhance code clarity and accessibility. They convey the meaning and purpose of specific sections of your extension's interface.

```html
<header>
    <h1>My Extension</h1>
</header>
```

Accessibility

Ensuring your extension's HTML is accessible to all users is a critical consideration. By following accessibility guidelines, you make your extension usable by individuals with disabilities. Use semantic elements, provide alternative text for images, and use ARIA attributes when necessary.

```html
<img src="image.jpg" alt="A descriptive alternative text">
<button aria-label="Close">X</button>
```

Understanding these HTML essentials will empower you to create well-structured and accessible user interfaces for your Chrome extensions. These fundamentals form the basis for building engaging and user-friendly extension interfaces.

Styling with CSS

CSS, or Cascading Style Sheets, plays a pivotal role in shaping the appearance of web content, including

Chrome extension interfaces. In this section, we'll delve into CSS fundamentals, selectors, properties, and best practices for effective styling.

Introduction to CSS

CSS is the language of style on the web. It allows you to control the presentation and layout of HTML elements, making web pages and extension interfaces visually appealing and user-friendly.

Selectors

Selectors are a fundamental concept in CSS. They determine which HTML elements will be affected by a style rule. Some common selectors include:

1. **Element Selectors**: Select all instances of a specific HTML element. For example, **p** selects all paragraphs.

2. **Class Selectors**: Select elements with a specific class attribute. For example, **.highlight** selects all elements with the class "highlight."

3. **ID Selectors**: Select a specific element by its unique ID attribute. For example, **#header** selects the element with the ID "header."

4. **Combination Selectors**: Combine multiple selectors to target specific elements more precisely. For example, **ul.navbar** selects unordered lists with the class "navbar."

Properties and Values

CSS properties determine the style aspect you want to change, while values specify how that change should be applied. Here are some essential CSS properties:

1. **Color**: **color** property sets the text color.

2. **Background Color**: **background-color** sets the background color.

3. **Font Size**: **font-size** controls text size.

4. **Margin and Padding**: **margin** creates space outside an element, while **padding** creates space inside.

5. **Border**: **border** defines the element's border properties.

Cascade and Specificity

CSS follows a cascade and specificity model, which determines the order in which conflicting styles are applied. Understanding this concept is crucial for resolving styling conflicts:

1. **Cascade**: Styles are applied in a specific order, with later styles potentially overriding earlier ones.

2. **Specificity**: Specificity refers to the weight of a style rule. More specific rules take precedence over less specific ones.

   For example, an inline style (**<p style="color: blue;">**) is more specific than a class selector (**p.special**) and will override it.

Styling Chrome Extension Interfaces

In Chrome extension development, CSS is instrumental in crafting visually appealing and user-friendly interfaces. Here's how CSS is commonly used in extension development:

Applying Styles

To apply CSS styles to HTML elements within your extension, you link an external CSS file or use inline styles. For example, to style a button:

```html
<button class="primary-button">Click Me</button>
```

```css
.primary-button {
    background-color: #3498db;
    color: #fff;
    padding: 10px 20px;
    border: none;
    cursor: pointer;
}
```

Box Model

Understanding the box model is crucial for controlling element dimensions and spacing. The box model consists of content, padding, border, and margin. Each component influences an element's overall size and appearance.

```css
/* Example of the box model */
.element {
    width: 200px;
    padding: 20px;
    border: 2px solid #333;
    margin: 10px;
}
```

Responsive Design

In the era of diverse devices and screen sizes, responsive design is essential. CSS media queries allow you to adjust styles based on the user's device, ensuring a seamless experience on both desktop and mobile devices.

```css
/* Example of a media query for responsiveness */
@media (max-width: 768px) {
    .element {
        font-size: 14px;
    }
}
```

Implementing CSS Best Practices

Maintaining a clean and efficient CSS codebase is vital for managing complex extension interfaces. Consider the following best practices:

Modularity

Break your CSS into manageable modules, with each module focusing on specific components or sections of your extension. This approach makes your code more organized and easier to maintain.

```css
/* Example of modular CSS */
.header {
    /* styles for the header section */
}

.button {
    /* styles for buttons */
}
```

Comments

Adding comments to your CSS code clarifies your intentions and makes it easier for you and others to understand the purpose of specific styles.

```css
/* Comment explaining a style rule */
.button {
    /* styles for buttons */
}
```

Performance

Optimize your CSS for performance by reducing redundancy and minimizing file size. Use 'tools like minification and compression to improve loading times.

With these CSS essentials and best practices in mind, you're well-prepared to style your Chrome extension interfaces effectively. CSS empowers you to create visually appealing and user-friendly user interfaces, enhancing the overall user experience.

JavaScript Fundamentals

JavaScript, often referred to as the "language of the web," is a versatile and powerful scripting language. It plays a pivotal role in enhancing user interactions and adding functionality to web pages and Chrome extensions. In this section, we'll delve into the fundamental concepts of JavaScript and its significance in extension development.

Introduction to JavaScript

JavaScript is a client-side scripting language used to make web pages and extensions interactive and dynamic. It allows you to manipulate HTML content, respond to user actions, and interact with external resources, such as APIs. Here are some key concepts:

Variables and Data Types

Variables are used to store data, and JavaScript supports various data types:

1. **Strings**: Used for text, enclosed in single or double quotes. For example: **"Hello, world!"**

2. **Numbers**: Represent both integers and floating-point numbers. For example: **42** or **3.14**

3. **Booleans**: Represent true or false values. For example: **true** or **false**

4. **Objects**: Complex data structures that can store multiple values. For example, an object representing a person might have properties like **name** and **age**.

Operators

JavaScript includes operators for performing operations on variables and values:

1. **Arithmetic Operators**: Used for basic mathematical operations, such as addition (**+**), subtraction (**-**), multiplication (*****), and division (**/**).

2. **Comparison Operators**: Used to compare values, such as equal to (==), not equal to (!=), greater than (>), and less than (<).

3. **Logical Operators**: Used for logical operations, such as **&&** (and), **||** (or), and **!** (not).

Functions and Control Flow

JavaScript uses functions to group and encapsulate code that can be executed when called. Control flow statements, such as **if**, **else**, and loops, determine how the code is executed:

Functions

A function is a block of code that can be called and executed. Functions can take parameters (inputs) and return values (outputs). Here's an example of a simple function:

```javascript
function greet(name) {
    return "Hello, " + name + "!";
}
```

Conditional Statements

Conditional statements allow you to execute code based on specific conditions. For example:

```javascript
if (age < 18) {
    alert("You are a minor.");
} else {
    alert("You are an adult.");
}
```

Loops

Loops are used for repetitive tasks. The **for** loop is a common choice for iterating over data or performing a specific action multiple times:

```javascript
for (let i = 0; i < 5; i++) {
    console.log("Iteration " + i);
}
```

Handling User Interactions with JavaScript

One of JavaScript's strengths is its ability to respond to user interactions. You can capture events like clicks, keystrokes, and mouse movements and execute code in response.

Event Handling

Event handlers are functions that respond to specific events. For example, to execute code when a button is clicked:

```javascript
document.getElementById("myButton").addEventListener("click", function() {
    alert("Button clicked!");
});
```

DOM Manipulation

The Document Object Model (DOM) represents the structure of an HTML document as a tree of objects.

JavaScript allows you to manipulate this tree, changing elements and their attributes dynamically.

```javascript
// Changing the text of an element
document.getElementById("myParagraph").textContent = "New text content";
```

Writing Efficient and Maintainable JavaScript Code

To develop high-quality Chrome extensions, it's essential to write JavaScript code that's efficient and maintainable:

Best Practices

- **Modularity**: Organize your code into reusable functions and modules for better maintainability.

- **Comments**: Add comments to explain complex logic or the purpose of functions and variables.

- **Debugging**: Use debugging tools to identify and fix errors efficiently.

With these JavaScript fundamentals in your toolbox, you're well-prepared to build interactive and dynamic Chrome extensions. JavaScript enables you to create extensions that respond to user actions, interact with web content, and deliver a seamless user experience.

Chapter 3: Anatomy of a Chrome Extension

In this chapter, we will embark on a detailed exploration of the internal structure and components that constitute a Chrome extension. Understanding the anatomy of a Chrome extension is crucial as it forms the foundation for creating effective, functional, and interactive extensions that enhance the browsing experience.

The Role of Manifest Files

At the core of every Chrome extension lies the manifest file. This file serves as the architectural blueprint for your extension, defining its structure, functionality, and permissions. Let's delve deeper into the pivotal aspects of manifest files:

1. **Extension Information**: Within the manifest file, metadata about the extension is specified. This includes vital details such as the extension's name, description, version, and author information. It serves as the face of your extension, providing users with essential information.

2. **Permissions**: Permissions are a key component of the manifest file. They determine which capabilities the extension is granted by the user. These permissions include accessing web pages, tabs, or the user's browsing history. Specifying permissions is crucial for ensuring that your extension functions as intended.

3. **Content Scripts**: Content scripts are JavaScript files that can be dynamically injected into web pages as they load. They act as a bridge between your extension and the content of web pages, enabling interactions and modifications. Content scripts are indispensable for creating dynamic and interactive extensions.

4. **Background Scripts**: Background scripts run in the background, invisible to the user. They serve as the central hub for managing extension-wide tasks. This includes handling events, managing data, and coordinating communication between different components of the extension.

5. **Popup and Options Pages**: The manifest file also specifies the HTML files that serve as the popup and options pages of the extension. These pages provide user interfaces for users to interact with the extension's features and configure settings according to their preferences.

The Significance of Background Scripts

Background scripts play a pivotal role in ensuring the functionality and responsiveness of a Chrome extension. These scripts operate silently in the background, managing essential tasks:

1. **Event Handling**: Background scripts are adept at listening for events triggered by user actions or web pages. For instance, they can respond to clicks on the extension icon, receive messages from content scripts, and orchestrate complex interactions.

2. **Data Management**: Often, background scripts are responsible for the storage and retrieval of extension-related data. This includes managing user preferences, settings, and data synchronization across different parts of the extension.

3. **Communication Hub**: Background scripts serve as the communication hub of the extension. They facilitate seamless interaction between various components, such as content scripts, popup pages, and options pages, ensuring a cohesive user experience.

Content Scripts and Their Vital Role

Content scripts are the dynamic actors within a Chrome extension. They are JavaScript files that can be dynamically injected into web pages as they load, serving as the vital link between your extension and the content of web pages:

1. **DOM Manipulation**: Content scripts wield the power to manipulate the Document Object Model (DOM) of a web page. This allows them to add, modify, or remove elements and content dynamically. It's through content scripts that your extension can exert influence over the visual aspects of web pages.

2. **Interacting with Page Scripts**: Content scripts can seamlessly communicate with JavaScript code running on the web page. This means your extension can interact with and harness the functionality of web pages, opening doors to a myriad of possibilities for enhancing user experiences.

3. **Isolation and Stability**: One key advantage of content scripts is their isolation from the web page's scripts. This isolation mitigates the risk of conflicts and ensures the stability of your extension. Content scripts operate independently, preventing them from interfering with the operation of the web page.

Creating User Interfaces: Popup and Options Pages

Popup and options pages are integral components that enhance the user experience of your Chrome extension:

1. **Popup Pages**: These pages make an appearance when users click on the extension icon in the Chrome toolbar. They provide quick access to essential features and information, offering a streamlined and convenient user experience. Popup pages are ideal for presenting concise and frequently used functionalities.

2. **Options Pages**: Options pages serve as the user's control centre, allowing them to configure and customize the behaviour of your extension. These pages provide a platform for users to tailor the extension according to their preferences, fostering a sense of ownership and personalization.

Best Practices for Managing Extension Files

Efficiently organizing and managing the files of your extension is crucial for development, maintenance, and collaboration:

1. **File Structure**: Adopt a structured and organized file hierarchy that categorizes files according to their types and functionalities. Separating HTML, CSS, JavaScript,

and other assets aids in the quick location and modification of specific components.

2. **Version Control**: Leverage version control systems like Git to meticulously track changes to your extension's codebase. This not only enables seamless collaboration but also ensures that you can confidently roll back changes if issues arise.

3. **Modularity**: Embrace modularity by dividing your code into reusable functions and modules. This approach fosters maintainability and reusability, allowing you to efficiently adapt and expand your extension.

4. **Performance Optimization**: Optimize the performance of your extension by reducing redundancy and optimizing code for efficiency. Minify and compress assets to improve loading times and user experience.

By comprehending the intricate anatomy of a Chrome extension, encompassing manifest files, background scripts, content scripts, and user interfaces, you equip yourself with the knowledge required to craft extensions that cater precisely to the needs of your users. A well-structured and well-managed extension architecture forms the cornerstone for developing engaging and feature-rich Chrome extensions.

Chapter 4: Building Your First Chrome Extension

In this chapter, we will delve deep into the process of creating your very first Chrome extension. Building a simple yet functional extension provides an excellent opportunity to gain hands-on experience and develop a profound understanding of extension development.

Step 1: Conceptualize Your Extension

Before embarking on your coding journey, it's paramount to have a crystal-clear concept in mind. This involves:

- **Problem Definition**: Identify a specific problem or need that your extension will address. A comprehensive understanding of the problem is the initial step towards crafting a solution that users will find invaluable.

- **Value Proposition**: Delve into how your extension will enrich users' experiences. Will it save them precious time, streamline complex processes, or enhance their browsing encounters? The value proposition must be articulated with precision.

Step 2: Set Up Your Development Environment

Prior to delving into code, it's imperative to ensure that your development environment is meticulously prepared:

- **Choosing a Code Editor**: Select a code editor that harmonizes with your workflow and preferences. Notable choices encompass Visual Studio Code, Sublime Text, and Atom.

- **Chrome Browser Installation**: Verify that the Chrome browser is installed on your computer. It constitutes an indispensable tool for testing and debugging your extension.

Step 3: Create a Dedicated Folder for Your Extension

Establish a dedicated folder for your extension project. This folder will serve as the epicenter for all your extension files, preserving the structural integrity of your project.

Step 4: Crafting the Manifest File

Each Chrome extension commences its journey with a manifest file christened **manifest.json**. Within this file, you'll articulate pivotal information about your extension:

- **Extension Name**: Convey the name of your extension with unmistakable clarity.

- **Version Number**: Concretely specify the current version of your extension.

- **Description**: Provide a concise, yet informative description of your extension's mission and functionality.

- **Permissions**: Enumerate the permissions your extension necessitates, whether it's accessing web pages or wielding control over bookmarks.

- **Icon Designation**: Confer distinct identities upon your extension through icons, including those adorning the toolbar and various user interface elements.

Step 5: Design and Create Icons

Design icons that will personify your extension. These icons shall be the visual ambassadors of your extension in the Chrome toolbar and other interfaces. You can opt for crafting custom icons employing graphic design software such as Adobe Illustrator or tap into the wealth of free icons available online.

Step 6: Developing HTML, CSS, and JavaScript

Depending on the intricacies of your extension's functionality, diligently craft the requisite HTML, CSS, and JavaScript files:

- **HTML**: Should your extension entail a popup interface, manifest an HTML file to bring it to life.

- **CSS**: Invoke CSS to bestow visual grace upon your extension's user interface elements.

- **JavaScript**: Engage in the art of scripting to breathe life into your extension, imparting it with the functionality it merits.

Step 7: Linking Files in the Manifest

Within your **manifest.json** file, solemnly specify the files you have meticulously crafted. For instance, if your extension boasts a popup page, illuminate its presence in the manifest under the **"browser_action"** section.

Step 8: Testing Your Extension

Navigate the path of testing your extension by traversing these steps:

1. Unfurl the Chrome browser.

2. Navigate to the Chrome Extensions citadel by invoking **chrome://extensions/** in the omnibox.

3. Activate Developer Mode via an authoritative toggle.

4. Click "Load unpacked" and escort your extension's project folder into the spotlight.

   Upon the completion of these steps, your extension's insignia shall grace the Chrome toolbar, opening the gates to interaction.

Step 9: Debugging and Troubleshooting

During your development odyssey, tribulations may arise. Confront them valiantly:

- **Console Logging**: Embed **console.log** statements within your JavaScript code, charting the course of execution and pinpointing errors.

- **Chrome Development Tools**: Enlist Chrome's eminent Developer Tools as your allies in the quest for debugging. They unveil the ability to scrutinize elements, peruse console output, and dissect network transactions.

- **Online Resources**: Harness the power of online forums, developer communities, and prodigious troves of documentation bestowed upon the realm of Chrome extension development. These sanctuaries harbour answers to the conundrums that beset you.

- **Testing Prowess**: Enact thorough tests upon your extension, unveiling its performance across an array of scenarios and environments.

Step 10: Refinement and Enhancement

Embark on a quest to garner user feedback, leveraging it as the cornerstone for enhancements:

- **User Feedback**: Assemble user feedback with diligence, acknowledging it as a precious resource. Users' insights can sculpt your extension's evolution.

- **Feature Expansion**: With your newfound expertise in extension development, contemplate augmenting your creation with additional features and functionalities.

By navigating these steps with finesse and embracing the art of troubleshooting, you'll construct a robust foundation upon which to erect your inaugural Chrome extension. While this example primarily showcases the creation of a simple extension, it serves as a springboard for the creation of intricate, feature-rich extensions tailored to the idiosyncratic demands of your user base.

Chapter 5: Interacting with Web Pages

Content Scripts: The Bridge to Web Pages

- In the realm of Chrome extensions, content scripts stand as a pivotal bridge between the extension's functionality and the dynamic web pages that users navigate daily. They play a vital role in enhancing the web experience and offering users valuable features seamlessly.

- *Understanding Content Scripts*: Content scripts are specialized JavaScript files meticulously crafted to interact harmoniously with web pages. These scripts operate in an isolated environment within the page, distinct from the extension's background scripts. This isolation ensures the prevention of conflicts with existing scripts on the web page, allowing for smooth coexistence.

- *Injection Process*: When a user ventures onto a web page, the content script springs into action, dynamically embedding itself into the page's code, all thanks to the rules and conditions meticulously outlined in the extension's manifest file. This precise injection ensures that the content script executes in the right context, unlocking its potential.

- *Access to DOM*: Content scripts wield the power to access the Document Object Model (DOM) of the web page. This capability empowers them to read, modify, or manipulate the page's elements and content dynamically. The DOM serves as a canvas for content scripts to craft interactive and customized experiences.

- *DOM Manipulation*: Chiefly, content scripts shine in their ability to manipulate the DOM of web pages. By employing JavaScript wizardry, they can add, modify, or remove elements from the page, transforming its visual appearance and interactive behavior.

- *Event Handling*: Content scripts are versatile in their interaction with web pages, allowing them to respond adeptly to user-triggered events such as clicks, key presses, or form submissions. This versatility endows Chrome extensions with the agility to create dynamic and responsive user interfaces.

In essence, content scripts are the unsung heroes of Chrome extensions, facilitating a harmonious coexistence between extensions and web pages. Their ability to seamlessly integrate and interact with web content opens a world of possibilities, allowing developers to create extensions that cater to users' unique needs and elevate their browsing experiences.

The Injection Process of Content Scripts in Chrome Extensions

The injection process of content scripts is a fundamental mechanism that empowers Chrome extensions to seamlessly interact with and modify web pages as users browse the internet. This process is at the core of enhancing user experiences and extending the functionality of web pages. In this chapter, we delve into the intricate details of how content scripts are injected into web pages and the crucial role they play.

Understanding Content Script Injection:

Content scripts are JavaScript files specifically crafted to interact with the Document Object Model (DOM) of web pages. They run in an isolated environment, distinct from the extension's background scripts, ensuring that they do not interfere with or conflict with the existing scripts on the web page. This isolation is a key design principle to maintain the stability and security of both the extension and the web page.

The injection process of content scripts occurs when a user navigates to a web page that matches the predefined criteria set in the extension's manifest file. These criteria typically include URL patterns or conditions that determine which web pages the content script should be injected into. When a matching page is detected, the extension dynamically injects the content script into the web page's context.

Rules Defined in the Manifest File:

The injection process begins with the rules and conditions specified in the extension's manifest file. These rules define when and where the content script should be injected. They can include:

1. **Matches**: URL patterns that specify the web pages where the content script should be injected. For example, an extension designed to work on all web pages might use the pattern **"<all_urls>"**.

2. **Excludes**: URL patterns to exclude specific web pages from the injection process. This is useful when the extension should not run on certain pages.

3. **Run At**: Determines when the content script should be executed in relation to the document's lifecycle. Common options include "document_start," "document_end," and "document_idle."

4. **CSS and JS Files**: Paths to CSS and JavaScript files that should be injected along with the content script. This allows the extension to apply custom styles or include additional functionality.

Dynamic Injection:

Once a user visits a web page that matches the defined criteria, the extension dynamically injects the content script into the page's context. This injection process is carefully orchestrated to ensure that the script operates within the right context, gaining access to the web page's DOM and resources.

The injection process is triggered by the browser, and the content script becomes an integral part of the web page's environment, capable of interacting with and modifying its content in real-time.

Access to the DOM:

With successful injection, the content script gains access to the Document Object Model (DOM) of the web page. The DOM represents the page's structure and content, including elements like text, images, forms, and more. This access is essential for content scripts to read, modify, or manipulate the page's elements and content dynamically.

Modifying Web Page Content:

Once injected and equipped with DOM access, the content script can execute JavaScript code to manipulate the web page's content. This can involve tasks like adding new elements, altering existing ones, or removing elements to tailor the page's structure to the extension's needs. For example, an extension might add a custom button to a web page or enhance the functionality of existing elements.

Understanding the Document Object Model (DOM)

The Document Object Model, often referred to as DOM, is a crucial concept in web development that defines the structure and organization of web documents, such as HTML or XML. It represents a web page as a hierarchical tree-like structure where each element on the page is a node in the tree.

Key Characteristics of the DOM:

1. **Tree Structure**: The DOM organizes a web page's content into a tree structure. The root of the tree is the document itself, and it branches out to include all elements on the page, such as headings, paragraphs, images, forms, and more.

2. **Nodes**: Each part of a web page, whether it's an entire document or a specific element like a paragraph or an

image, is represented as a node in the DOM tree. These nodes can be manipulated programmatically using languages like JavaScript.

3. **Hierarchical**: The DOM tree is hierarchical, meaning that nodes are organized in a parent-child relationship. For instance, an HTML document may have a **<body>** element as a parent node, with multiple **<p>** elements as its children.

4. **Access and Manipulation**: Developers can access and manipulate the content and structure of a web page by interacting with the DOM through programming languages like JavaScript. This allows for dynamic web pages and interactive user experiences.

5. **Synchronization**: The DOM is closely synchronized with the web page it represents. If changes are made to the DOM, such as adding new elements or modifying existing ones, those changes are reflected immediately in the displayed web page.

Use Cases of the DOM:

- **Dynamic Content**: Web developers use the DOM to create dynamic web pages where content can change without requiring a full page reload. This is commonly seen in modern web applications.

- **Interactivity**: DOM manipulation allows for interactive features such as form validation, real-time updates, and user interface enhancements.

- **Accessibility**: The DOM is crucial for making web content accessible to screen readers and other assistive technologies, as it provides a structured way to access and interpret web page content.

Access to DOM: Empowering Chrome Extensions

Access to the Document Object Model (DOM) is a cornerstone of the capabilities of Chrome extensions. It is through this access that extensions can interact with and manipulate the content of web pages, enhancing user experiences and extending the functionality of websites. In this section, we'll delve into the significance of DOM access for Chrome extensions and explore how it empowers developers to create feature-rich and interactive extensions.

The DOM: A Blueprint of Web Pages

The Document Object Model is a hierarchical representation of the structure and content of a web page. It provides a programmatic interface that allows scripts, like those in Chrome extensions, to interact with web page elements such as text, images, forms, links, and more. Think of it as a blueprint of a web page's structure.

Why DOM Access Matters for Extensions:

1. **Reading and Retrieving Information:** Chrome extensions often need to extract data or information from web pages. DOM access enables them to locate specific elements and retrieve data from them. For example, an extension designed to track prices on e-commerce websites can access the DOM to extract product prices.

2. **Modifying Content:** Beyond reading, extensions can modify the content of web pages. They can add new elements, change text, alter styles, or even remove elements from the DOM. This capability allows extensions to customize web pages to suit user preferences or inject additional functionality.

3. **Interactivity:** DOM access enables Chrome extensions to add interactivity to web pages. They can attach event listeners to elements, respond to user actions like clicks or form submissions, and create dynamic and responsive user interfaces.

4. **Enhancing User Experience:** By leveraging DOM access, extensions can enhance the overall user experience of websites. They can add features like tooltips, interactive widgets, or visual enhancements that provide value to users.

How DOM Access Works in Extensions:

DOM access in Chrome extensions is facilitated through content scripts. Content scripts are JavaScript files that are injected into web pages based on predefined criteria in the extension's manifest file. Once injected, these scripts operate within the context of the web page, gaining full access to its DOM.

Selecting DOM Elements:

One of the primary tasks of content scripts is selecting DOM elements. This is done using JavaScript selectors, which can target elements based on various criteria, such as their IDs, classes, attributes, or even their position within the DOM.

Libraries like jQuery are often used to simplify element selection and manipulation.

Modifying Content:

With access to selected DOM elements, extensions can modify the content or appearance of web pages. They can change the text within elements, apply CSS styles, insert new elements, or remove existing ones. This capability allows extensions to tailor the presentation of web pages according to user preferences.

Event Handling:

Event handling is another vital aspect of DOM access. Extensions can attach event listeners to DOM elements, enabling them to respond to user interactions. For instance, an extension could add a click event listener to a button on a web page and perform a specific action when the button is clicked.

Asynchronous Actions:

In some cases, extensions may need to perform asynchronous actions, such as making HTTP requests or fetching data from external sources. DOM access allows them to trigger and manage these actions within the context of the web page seamlessly.

Security Considerations:

While DOM access empowers extensions, it also raises security concerns. Extensions must be mindful of potential risks, such as cross-site scripting (XSS) vulnerabilities. Chrome's security mechanisms, including Content Security

Policies (CSPs), aim to mitigate these risks by controlling which scripts can be executed on a page.

DOM Manipulation in Chrome Extensions: Transforming Web Pages Dynamically

DOM manipulation is a powerful technique employed by Chrome extensions to dynamically alter the structure and content of web pages. It's a fundamental aspect of extension development that allows developers to customize web pages, enhance user experiences, and add valuable functionalities. In this comprehensive exploration, we'll delve into the art of DOM manipulation within Chrome extensions, uncovering its significance, techniques, and best practices.

The Significance of DOM Manipulation

1. **Customization**: DOM manipulation enables extensions to customize web pages to suit user preferences. Elements can be added, removed, or modified, tailoring the appearance and functionality of websites.

2. **Interactivity**: Extensions can use DOM manipulation to add interactive elements to web pages, such as buttons, forms, or widgets. This interactivity enhances user engagement and extends the functionality of websites.

3. **Content Augmentation**: Extensions can inject additional content into web pages. This could be anything from tooltips and information panels to advertising blockers and translation tools, enriching the user experience.

4. **Data Extraction**: DOM manipulation allows extensions to extract data from web pages. For instance, a price comparison extension can locate and retrieve product prices from e-commerce sites.

Effective DOM Manipulation Techniques

Efficient DOM manipulation is crucial for creating extensions that interact seamlessly with web pages. Here are some key techniques to master:

⚓ Selecting Elements

When building Chrome extensions, you often need to interact with specific elements on a web page. This may include buttons, input fields, links, or any other HTML elements. Here are some common methods to select elements:

1. **getElementById**: This method selects an element by its unique **id** attribute. Since IDs must be unique within an HTML document, this is the fastest way to access a specific element.

```javascript
// Example: Select an element with the id "myButton"
const buttonElement = document.getElementById("myButton");
```

2. **getElementsByClassName**: Use this method to select elements that share a common class name. It returns a collection of elements, allowing you to work with multiple elements at once.

```javascript
// Example: Select all elements with the class "info"
const infoElements = document.getElementsByClassName("info");
```

3. **getElementsByTagName**: This method targets elements based on their HTML tag name. It's useful when you want to select all elements of a particular type.

```javascript
// Example: Select all <a> elements (links)
const linkElements = document.getElementsByTagName("a");
```

4. **QuerySelector**: This versatile method allows you to use CSS-style selectors to precisely target elements. It returns the first matching element.

```javascript
// Example: Select the first element with class "important"
const importantElement = document.querySelector(".important");
```

5. **querySelectorAll**: Similar to **querySelector**, but it selects all matching elements and returns them as a Node List.

```javascript
// Example: Select all elements with the class "highlight"
const highlightedElements = document.querySelectorAll(".highlight");
```

❖ *Examples of Element Selection*

Let's walk through some practical examples of selecting elements using these methods:

1. **Selecting by ID**:

Suppose you want to select a button with the ID "submitButton" and change its text color:

```javascript
const submitButton = document.getElementById("submitButton");
submitButton.style.color = "blue";
```

2. **Selecting by Class:**

If you want to select all elements with the class "info" and add a border to each of them:

```javascript
const infoElements = document.getElementsByClassName("info");
for (const element of infoElements) {
  element.style.border = "1px solid gray";
}
```

3. **Selecting by Tag Name:**

To select all anchor tags (**<a>**) on a page and update their href attributes:

```javascript
const linkElements = document.getElementsByTagName("a");
for (const link of linkElements) {
  link.href = "https://example.com";
}
```

4. **Selecting with Query Selector:**

If you want to select the first element with the class "important" and hide it:

```javascript
const importantElement = document.querySelector(".important");
importantElement.style.display = "none";
```

5. **Selecting Multiple Elements with Query Selector All**:

To select all elements with the class "highlight" and set their background colour to yellow:

```javascript
const highlightedElements = document.querySelectorAll(".highlight");
for (const element of highlightedElements) {
  element.style.backgroundColor = "yellow";
}
```

These examples demonstrate how to use different selection methods to target specific elements on a web page. Understanding when and how to use these methods is essential for effective DOM manipulation in your Chrome extensions.

⊹ Modifying Content

Modifying content on web pages is a common task for Chrome extensions. Whether you want to inject additional information, change the appearance of elements, or customize the content, these techniques will help you achieve your goals:

1. **Updating InnerHTML**:

One of the simplest ways to modify content is by updating the **innerHTML** property of an element. This allows you to change the HTML content within an element. For example, if you have a paragraph with the id "message," you can change its text as follows:

```javascript
// Select the element
const messageElement = document.getElementById("message");

// Update its content
messageElement.innerHTML = "New content here!";
```

This can be particularly useful for injecting new HTML elements or formatting.

2. **Updating Text Content**:

If you only want to change the text content of an element, you can use the **textContent** property. It ensures that any HTML tags within the content are treated as text and not parsed as HTML:

```javascript
// Select the element
const paragraphElement = document.getElementById("paragraph");

// Update its text content
paragraphElement.textContent = "This is the updated text.";
```

This is helpful when you want to modify plain text within elements.

3. **Creating and Appending Elements**:

To add new elements to a web page, you can create them dynamically and append them to the DOM. For example, to add a new **<div>** element with some text content:

```javascript
// Create a new div element
const newDiv = document.createElement("div");

// Set its content
newDiv.textContent = "This is a new div.";

// Append it to an existing element
document.body.appendChild(newDiv);
```

This allows you to inject custom elements into the page.

4. **Modifying Attributes**:

You can also modify attributes of elements, such as '**src**' for images or '**href**' for links. For example, to change the source of an image:

```javascript
// Select an image element
const imageElement = document.getElementById("myImage");

// Change its source
imageElement.src = "new-image.jpg";
```

This is useful for updating media content or links dynamically.

❖ *Examples of Content Modification*

Let's explore some practical examples of modifying content on a web page using these techniques:

1. **Injecting Additional Content**:

Suppose you want to inject a new paragraph with a message into a page:

```javascript
// Create a new paragraph element
const newParagraph = document.createElement("p");

// Set its content
newParagraph.textContent = "This is additional content injected by the exte

// Append it to the body
document.body.appendChild(newParagraph);
```

2. **Updating Existing Text**:

If you want to update the text content of an existing element with the id "notification":

```javascript
// Select the element
const notificationElement = document.getElementById("notification");

// Update its text content
notificationElement.textContent = "New notification message.";
```

3. **Changing Image Source**:

To change the source of an image with the id "profileImage":

```javascript
// Select the image element
const profileImageElement = document.getElementById("profileImage");

// Change its source
profileImageElement.src = "new-profile-image.jpg";
```

These examples demonstrate how to effectively modify content on web pages using JavaScript within your Chrome extension. Whether it's injecting new content, updating existing text, or changing attributes, these techniques empower you to customize the browsing experience for users.

⚓ Adding and Removing Elements

Adding and removing elements on web pages is a powerful feature for Chrome extensions. It enables you to create interactive and dynamic user interfaces or streamline content. Here are some techniques and examples of how to add and remove elements:

1. **Creating New Elements**:

   To add new elements to a web page, you can create them dynamically using JavaScript. For instance, let's say you want to add a new button with an event listener:

```javascript
// Create a new button element
const newButton = document.createElement("button");

// Set its attributes
newButton.textContent = "Click me";
newButton.addEventListener("click", () => {
  alert("Button clicked!");
});

// Append it to an existing element (e.g., the body)
document.body.appendChild(newButton);
```

   This code creates a new button element, sets its text and click event listener, and appends it to the document's body.

2. **Removing Elements**:

Removing elements from a web page is equally important. You can select an element and remove it programmatically. Suppose you want to remove an existing element with the id "removeMe":

```javascript
// Select the element to be removed
const elementToRemove = document.getElementById("removeMe");

// Check if the element exists before removing it
if (elementToRemove) {
  elementToRemove.remove();
}
```

This code first checks if the element exists and then removes it from the DOM.

❖ **Elements Examples of Adding and Removing**
   Let's explore some practical examples of adding and removing elements on a web page using these techniques:

1. **Adding Form Elements**:

Imagine you want to create a simple form with input fields dynamically:

```javascript
// Create a form element
const formElement = document.createElement("form");

// Create an input field
const inputElement = document.createElement("input");
inputElement.type = "text";
inputElement.placeholder = "Enter your name";

// Create a submit button
const submitButton = document.createElement("button");
submitButton.type = "submit";
submitButton.textContent = "Submit";

// Append elements to the form
formElement.appendChild(inputElement);
formElement.appendChild(submitButton);

// Append the form to an existing element (e.g., a div)
const container = document.getElementById("formContainer");
container.appendChild(formElement);
```

This code dynamically creates a form with an input field and a submit button within an existing div with the id "formContainer."

2. **Removing Unwanted Content**:

Suppose you want to remove ads from a webpage based on their CSS class:

```javascript
// Select all elements with the "ad" class
const ads = document.querySelectorAll(".ad");

// Remove each ad element
ads.forEach((ad) => {
  ad.remove();
});
```

This code identifies all elements with the "ad" class and removes them from the page.

These examples illustrate how you can effectively add new elements for enhanced functionality or remove unwanted content to improve the user experience on web pages using your Chrome extension. This dynamic manipulation of elements empowers you to create tailored and interactive web experiences.

⬇ Event Handling in Chrome Extensions

Event handling refers to the process of detecting and responding to events that occur during the interaction between a user and a web page. Chrome extensions often use event handling to create dynamic and interactive features. Here are some key aspects of event handling in Chrome extensions:

1. **Types of Events**:

   Events can vary widely, from mouse interactions (e.g., clicks and hovers) to keyboard actions (e.g., keypresses) and form submissions. Each type of event serves a specific purpose and can trigger custom actions in your extension.

2. **Event Listeners**:

Event listeners are functions that are bound to specific elements on a web page. They listen for a particular type of event and execute a predefined action when that event occurs. You can attach event listeners to HTML elements, ensuring that your extension responds appropriately to user interactions.

3. **Event Propagation**:

In the DOM (Document Object Model), events propagate or bubble up through the hierarchy of elements. Understanding event propagation is crucial because it determines the order in which event handlers are triggered when multiple elements are nested.

4. **Asynchronous Actions**:

Some interactions with web pages, such as making AJAX requests, may involve asynchronous actions. Effective event handling should account for such scenarios, ensuring that your extension remains responsive.

❖ *Examples of Event Handling*

Let's explore some practical examples of event handling in Chrome extensions:

1. **Click Event Handling**:

Suppose you want to create an extension that highlights the text when the user clicks on it. You can achieve this with event handling:

```javascript
// Find the element you want to make clickable
const textElement = document.getElementById("clickableText");

// Attach a click event listener to it
textElement.addEventListener("click", () => {
  // Change the text color to red
  textElement.style.color = "red";
});
```

In this example, when the user clicks on an element with the id "clickableText," the event listener changes the text color to red.

2. **Form Submission Handling**:

Let's say you want to create a form submission extension that logs user submissions:

```javascript
// Find the form element
const formElement = document.getElementById("submissionForm");

// Attach a form submission event listener
formElement.addEventListener("submit", (event) => {
  // Prevent the default form submission
  event.preventDefault();

  // Access form data
  const formData = new FormData(formElement);
  const username = formData.get("username");
  const email = formData.get("email");

  // Log the data
  console.log(`Username: ${username}, Email: ${email}`);
});
```

Here, the event listener prevents the default form submission, extracts form data, and logs it when the user submits the form.

3. **Key Press Event Handling**:

Suppose you want to create a simple extension that triggers an action when the user presses a specific key, like the "Enter" key:

```javascript
// Attach a key press event listener to the document
document.addEventListener("keypress", (event) => {
  // Check if the pressed key is "Enter" (key code 13)
  if (event.keyCode === 13) {
    // Perform your desired action
    alert("Enter key pressed!");
  }
});
```

In this case, the extension listens for keypress events and triggers an alert when the "Enter" key is pressed.

These examples demonstrate how event handling can be applied in Chrome extensions to create interactive and responsive features. Event listeners are essential tools for enhancing user interactions and extending the functionality of your extensions on web pages.

Advanced Techniques in Web Interaction

To take your web interaction capabilities to the next level, consider these advanced techniques:

1) Cross-origin Communication:

Cross-origin communication is a crucial aspect of Chrome extension development when interacting with web pages hosted on different domains. Browsers typically enforce the same-origin policy to ensure security, which restricts web pages from making requests to a different domain than the one that served the web page. However, Chrome extensions often need to access resources from various origins to provide enhanced functionality.

Here are some essential concepts and techniques for cross-origin communication, along with examples:

1. Cross-Origin XMLHttpRequest (XHR):

- The XMLHttpRequest object is a core part of JavaScript used to make HTTP requests from web pages.

- Example: In a Chrome extension, you can use XHR to fetch data from an external API hosted on a different domain.

```javascript
var xhr = new XMLHttpRequest();
xhr.open("GET", "https://api.example.com/data", true);
xhr.onreadystatechange = function () {
  if (xhr.readyState == 4 && xhr.status == 200) {
    var response = JSON.parse(xhr.responseText);
    // Process the data from the external domain
  }
};
xhr.send();
```

2. CORS (Cross-Origin Resource Sharing):

- CORS is a security feature implemented on the server-side to define which origins are allowed to access specific resources.

- Example: A server can include CORS headers in its response to permit cross-origin requests from specific origins.

```javascript
// Server-side code (e.g., in Node.js with Express)
const express = require("express");
const app = express();

app.use((req, res, next) => {
  res.header("Access-Control-Allow-Origin", "https://your-extension-domain.c
  res.header("Access-Control-Allow-Methods", "GET, POST, OPTIONS");
  res.header("Access-Control-Allow-Headers", "Content-Type");
  next();
});

// REST of your server code

app.listen(3000);
```

3. Browser Extensions APIs:

- Chrome provides APIs like **chrome.runtime.connect** and **chrome.runtime.sendMessage** to enable communication between content scripts and background scripts, even when dealing with cross-origin pages.

- Example: A content script can send a message to a background script requesting data from a cross-origin web page.

```javascript
// Content script
chrome.runtime.sendMessage({ action: "fetchData" }, (response) => {
  // Handle the response from the background script
});
```

Mastering cross-origin communication is essential for Chrome extension developers to build versatile extensions capable of securely interacting with web pages from various domains. These techniques empower developers to enhance user experiences while adhering to web security principles.

3)Content Script Lifecycle :

Understanding the content script lifecycle is crucial for Chrome extension developers. Content scripts are JavaScript files that run in the context of a web page, and they have their own lifecycle that determines when they are injected, executed, and unloaded.

Injection of Content Scripts: Content scripts are dynamically injected into web pages by the Chrome extension when certain conditions defined in the extension's manifest file are met. These conditions can include matching specific URLs or URL patterns. Content scripts are injected after the web page's DOM has been constructed but before the page has fully loaded. This allows them to interact with the page's elements and content as soon as they are available.

Execution and Persistence: Once injected, content scripts continue to execute as long as the web page remains open and matches the defined conditions. They can manipulate the DOM, handle events, and communicate with background scripts or other parts of the extension. Content scripts persist even when the user navigates to different pages within the same website or domain, as long as the conditions for injection are met.

Unloading Content Scripts: Content scripts are unloaded when the user navigates to a different website or when the tab is closed. This unloading is automatic and is designed to free up resources and prevent unnecessary script execution.

Example: Suppose you have a Chrome extension that enhances the functionality of social media websites by adding additional features. You define a content script in your manifest file to inject your JavaScript code into pages with URLs matching social media sites like Facebook, Twitter, and Instagram.

```
// manifest.json
{
  "manifest_version": 3,
  "name": "Social Enhancer",
  "version": "1.0",
  "permissions": ["activeTab"],
  "content_scripts": [
    {
      "matches": ["*://www.facebook.com/*", "*://twitter.com/*", "*://www.i
      "js": ["content.js"]
    }
  ],
  "background": {
    "service_worker": "background.js"
  },
  "action": {
    "default_popup": "popup.html",
    "default_icon": {
      "16": "images/icon16.png",
      "48": "images/icon48.png",
      "128": "images/icon128.png"
    }
  }
}
```

In this example, when a user navigates to Facebook, Twitter, or Instagram, the content script (**content.js**) is injected into the page, allowing it to modify the DOM and add the desired features. The content script persists as long as the user is on one of these social media sites and is automatically unloaded when they leave the site.

4) Performance Optimization:

Performance optimization is a critical aspect of developing Chrome extensions that interact with web pages. Efficient extensions not only provide a smoother user experience but also consume fewer system resources, enhancing overall browser performance.

Here are some key techniques and examples for optimizing the performance of your content scripts:

1. **Lazy Loading:** Load your content scripts only when they are needed. You can achieve this by specifying "run_at" in your manifest file as "document_end" or programmatically injecting content scripts when a user interacts with your extension. This reduces initial page load times.

```json
// Manifest.json
{
  "content_scripts": [
    {
      "matches": ["*://example.com/*"],
      "js": ["content.js"],
      "run_at": "document_end" // Delay script execution
    }
  ]
}
```

2. **Efficient DOM Traversal:** Minimize unnecessary DOM traversal. Use methods like **querySelector** or **getElementById** to select specific elements efficiently instead of traversing the entire DOM tree repeatedly. This reduces CPU and memory usage.

```javascript
// Efficient DOM traversal
const element = document.querySelector("#targetElement");
```

3. **Batching and Debouncing:** When handling user interactions, batch and debounce event handlers to avoid excessive function calls. This is especially useful when dealing with frequent events like scroll or resize.

```javascript
// Debounce scroll event
function debounce(func, wait) {
  let timeout;
  return function () {
    const context = this,
      args = arguments;
    clearTimeout(timeout);
    timeout = setTimeout(function () {
      func.apply(context, args);
    }, wait);
  };
}
```

4. **Minimize Script Size:** Reduce the size of your content scripts by eliminating unnecessary code and dependencies. Use minification and compression tools to optimize script files.

5. **Memory Management:** Be mindful of memory leaks. Remove event listeners and references to DOM elements when they are no longer needed to prevent memory build up.

6. **Throttle AJAX Requests:** If your extension makes AJAX requests to external servers, consider throttling these requests to prevent overloading the server and to conserve system resources.

7. **Caching:** Cache data when appropriate. If your extension retrieves data from external sources, store it locally to reduce redundant requests.

8. **Use Web Workers:** For CPU-intensive tasks, consider using web workers to offload processing from the main thread, preventing UI freezes and improving overall responsiveness.

Performance optimization is an ongoing process. Regularly test your extension's performance and profile its resource usage to identify areas for improvement. By following these optimization techniques and being mindful of resource usage, you can create Chrome extensions that provide a smoother user experience and are more efficient in terms of system resource utilization.

5) Handling Dynamic Pages :

Handling dynamic web pages is crucial for Chrome extensions, as many modern websites use AJAX requests or single-page application (SPA) frameworks to load content dynamically without requiring full page reloads. Here are some strategies and examples for effectively dealing with dynamic pages in your extension:

1. **Event Listening:** Observe DOM mutations and listen for events triggered by dynamic page changes. You can use the '**MutationObserver**' API to monitor DOM mutations and execute your code accordingly.

```javascript
// Example using MutationObserver to detect dynamic content changes
const observer = new MutationObserver((mutations) => {
  mutations.forEach((mutation) => {
    if (mutation.type === 'childList') {
      // Handle dynamic content change here
    }
  });
});
const config = { childList: true, subtree: true };
observer.observe(document.body, config);
```

2. **Content Scripts Reload:** Some SPAs load content dynamically while navigating within the same page. In such cases, you may need to reinject your content scripts when the page's URL changes.

```javascript
// Example of reinjecting content scripts on URL change
chrome.runtime.onMessage.addListener((message, sender, sendResponse) => {
  if (message.action === 'pageChanged') {
    // Reinject content scripts here
  }
});
```

3. **AJAX Event Handling:** Intercept AJAX requests made by the page and inject your logic to process the responses or perform additional actions.

```javascript
// Example of intercepting AJAX requests
const xhrOpen = window.XMLHttpRequest.prototype.open;
window.XMLHttpRequest.prototype.open = function (method, url) {
  this.addEventListener('load', function () {
    if (url.includes('example.com/api')) {
      // Handle the AJAX response here
    }
  });
  xhrOpen.apply(this, arguments);
};
```

4. **Timers and Intervals:** Sometimes, dynamic content may load after a delay. Use **'setTimeout'** or **'setInterval'** to periodically check for the presence of the content and act accordingly.

```javascript
// Example using setTimeout to check for dynamic content
const checkForDynamicContent = () => {
  const dynamicElement = document.querySelector('.dynamic-element');
  if (dynamicElement) {
    // Handle the dynamic content here
  } else {
    setTimeout(checkForDynamicContent, 1000); // Check again after 1 second
  }
};
checkForDynamicContent();
```

5. **Message Passing:** Communicate between content scripts and background scripts to coordinate actions when dynamic changes occur. This is especially useful when handling complex dynamic interactions.

```javascript
// Example of message passing between content scripts and background script
// Content script
chrome.runtime.sendMessage({ action: 'dynamicChangeDetected' });

// Background script
chrome.runtime.onMessage.addListener((message, sender, sendResponse) => {
  if (message.action === 'dynamicChangeDetected') {
    // Handle the dynamic change
  }
});
```

By employing these strategies and adapting them to your extension's specific needs, you can effectively handle dynamic pages, ensuring that your Chrome extension continues to provide valuable functionality even on websites with complex, dynamic content loading mechanisms.

6)Content Security Policies (CSPs):

Content Security Policy (CSP) is a crucial security feature that helps protect websites and web applications from various types of attacks, such as cross-site scripting (XSS) and data injection. CSP allows website administrators to define and enforce a set of rules that dictate which sources of content are trusted and can be executed or displayed on a web page. By specifying these policies, CSP mitigates the risk of unauthorized script execution and helps maintain the integrity of a website's code. Implementing CSP is a best practice for enhancing web application security and ensuring that only trusted resources are loaded, reducing the potential for security vulnerabilities.

.

Chapter 6: Extension Functionality

In this chapter, we will explore the core functionalities of Chrome extensions. These functionalities include making API requests, handling data, and organizing your code to create a well-structured and efficient extension.

Making API Requests

API (Application Programming Interface) requests are at the heart of many Chrome extensions. They enable your extension to interact with external services, retrieve data, and perform various actions. Understanding how to make API requests is essential for building dynamic and data-driven extensions

Introduction to APIs: Unleashing the Power of Integration

In the world of technology, APIs, or Application Programming Interfaces, have emerged as the glue that connects disparate systems, enabling them to work together harmoniously. APIs are the unsung heroes of the digital age, facilitating seamless communication and interaction between software applications, services, and platforms. In this chapter, we'll embark on a journey to demystify APIs, exploring what they are, how they work, and their pivotal role in modern software development.

Understanding APIs

At its core, an API is a set of rules and protocols that allows one piece of software to interact with another. Think of it as a mediator, bridging the gap between different programs, services, or even devices, enabling them to share data and functionality. APIs are like the universal language of the digital realm, allowing applications to request and exchange information effortlessly.

The Language of Interactions

Imagine a scenario where you want to book a flight online. You visit a travel booking website, enter your destination and travel dates, and hit the search button. Behind the scenes, the website communicates with multiple airline databases, retrieves flight information, and presents you with a list of available options. This exchange of data and actions is possible because of APIs.

APIs define how requests and responses should be structured, specifying the data format, authentication method, and available functions. They act as intermediaries, ensuring that the website can speak the same language as the airline databases, despite their differences in technologies and infrastructures.

Types of APIs

APIs come in various forms, each tailored to specific use cases:

1. **Web APIs**: These are perhaps the most common and accessible APIs. Web APIs, also known as HTTP APIs or RESTful APIs, operate over the internet and use the HTTP protocol to send and receive data. They are the backbone of many web and mobile applications,

providing access to services like social media platforms, payment gateways, and weather forecasts.

2. **Library APIs**: Some APIs are bundled as libraries or software development kits (SDKs) that developers can include in their applications. These libraries provide pre-built functions and tools for specific tasks, such as image processing, machine learning, or hardware control.

3. **Operating System APIs**: OS-level APIs expose the underlying functions and capabilities of an operating system. Developers use them to create software that interacts with the operating system's features, such as file management, hardware access, and user interface elements.

4. **Hardware APIs**: These APIs allow software applications to communicate directly with hardware devices like sensors, cameras, or printers. They enable the development of applications that harness the full potential of hardware components.

APIs in Action

APIs empower developers to tap into the wealth of functionalities offered by third-party services, extending the capabilities of their own applications. For instance, a weather forecasting app may rely on an external weather API to provide real-time weather updates. Similarly, social media integration, online payment processing, and location-based services all rely on APIs to function seamlessly.

The API Ecosystem

The API landscape is vast and continually evolving. Many organizations offer public APIs, allowing developers to access their services and data, often in exchange for adhering to specific usage terms and limits. Additionally, APIs play a crucial role in microservices architectures, where individual software components communicate via APIs, creating scalable and maintainable systems.

In summary, APIs are the building blocks of modern software development, enabling interoperability, integration, and the creation of innovative applications. As we delve deeper into this chapter, we'll explore the mechanics of API requests, authentication methods, and best practices for harnessing the power of APIs in your Chrome extension development journey.

Demystifying HTTP Requests: The Backbone of Web Communication

In the realm of web development and data exchange, HTTP (Hypertext Transfer Protocol) requests stand as the cornerstone of communication between clients and servers. These requests facilitate the retrieval and exchange of data, enabling the web to function as the dynamic and interconnected platform we know today. In this exploration, we will unravel the intricacies of HTTP requests, understanding their types, components, and significance in web interactions.

The Nature of HTTP Requests

At its core, an HTTP request is a message sent from a client, typically a web browser, to a web server. This message conveys the client's intent to retrieve or manipulate data. The server, in turn, processes the request and sends an HTTP response, containing the requested data or an acknowledgment of the client's action.

The Anatomy of an HTTP Request

An HTTP request consists of several essential components:

1. **HTTP Method**: This signifies the action the client wishes to perform. Common HTTP methods include:

    - **GET**: Requests data from the server.

    - **POST**: Submits data to the server for processing.

    - **PUT**: Updates existing data on the server.

    - **DELETE**: Requests the removal of data from the server.

2. **URL (Uniform Resource Locator)**: The URL specifies the resource's location on the server, providing a unique address for the request. It typically includes the protocol (e.g., "https://"), domain name, and path to the resource.

3. **Headers**: HTTP headers contain metadata about the request, including information about the client, accepted data formats (e.g., JSON or XML), and any authentication tokens.

4. **Body (Optional)**: Some requests, like POST or PUT, may include a request body containing data to be sent to the

server. This is often used for form submissions or API calls.

Types of HTTP Requests

HTTP requests fall into several categories, with the most common being:

1. **GET Request**: A GET request is used to retrieve data from the server. It is a read-only operation and does not modify server data. When you visit a webpage, your browser sends GET requests to fetch the HTML, CSS, JavaScript, and other assets needed to render the page.

2. **POST Request**: POST requests are employed to send data to the server for processing. This is commonly used for submitting forms, sending data to an API, or making database updates.

3. **PUT Request**: PUT requests update or replace existing data on the server with the provided data. It is often used for updating resource properties or saving a new version of a resource.

4. **DELETE Request**: As the name suggests, DELETE requests instruct the server to remove a specific resource. These requests are commonly used in RESTful APIs for resource deletion.

The Client-Server Dance

When a user interacts with a web application, a series of HTTP requests and responses form the backbone of the experience. For instance, when you click a link on a webpage, your browser sends a GET request to the server hosting the linked page. The server processes the request, retrieves the requested webpage, and sends it back as an HTTP response. This process repeats as you navigate through the web, with each interaction being a choreographed HTTP request-response dance.

Status Codes and Responses

HTTP responses from the server include a status code, which indicates the outcome of the request. Common status codes include:

- 200 (OK): The request was successful.

- 201 (Created): A new resource was successfully created.

- 404 (Not Found): The requested resource was not found.

- 500 (Internal Server Error): An error occurred on the server.

Security and Authentication

HTTP requests can be secured using HTTPS (HTTP Secure), which encrypts the data exchanged between the client and server, ensuring confidentiality and data integrity. Authentication mechanisms, such as API keys, tokens, and OAuth, are used to verify the identity of clients and control access to protected resources In conclusion, HTTP requests are the linchpin of web communication, facilitating the exchange of data and actions between clients and servers. Understanding the different types of requests, their components, and the significance of status codes is crucial for web developers and anyone navigating the digital landscape.

Mastering Data Retrieval: A Guide to Using the Fetch API

In the ever-evolving landscape of web development, data retrieval and interaction with remote resources play a pivotal role. The Fetch API, introduced as part of the modern JavaScript ecosystem, has emerged as a powerful tool for making HTTP requests, fetching data, and handling responses seamlessly. In this exploration, we will delve into the world of the Fetch API, understanding its core concepts, usage, and the benefits it brings to web developers.

What is the Fetch API?

The Fetch API is a built-in JavaScript interface that allows web developers to make asynchronous HTTP requests to servers, fetch data, and handle responses in a straightforward and efficient manner. Unlike its predecessor, 'XMLHttpRequest', the Fetch API is designed with a more user-friendly and promise-based approach, making it a natural fit for modern web development.

Fetching Data with Fetch

The core function of the Fetch API is to retrieve data from a specified URL. To initiate a fetch operation, you simply create a Fetch request by providing the URL as an argument. Here's a basic example of how to use Fetch to fetch data from a remote server:

```javascript
fetch('https://api.example.com/data')
  .then(response => {
    if (!response.ok) {
      throw new Error('Network response was not ok');
    }
    return response.json(); // Parse the response as JSON
  })
  .then(data => {
    // Handle the retrieved data
    console.log(data);
  })
  .catch(error => {
    // Handle errors
    console.error('Fetch error:', error);
  });
```

Promises and Chaining

One of the notable features of the Fetch API is its reliance on Promises for handling asynchronous operations. In the example above, you see a chain of **.then()** and **.catch()** methods. This pattern allows you to handle the response when it's successful and catch errors when they occur. It provides a clean and intuitive way to structure asynchronous code.

Customizing Fetch Requests

The Fetch API offers flexibility when it comes to customizing requests. You can specify request headers, HTTP methods, and even pass data in the request body. Here's an example of customizing a Fetch request:

```javascript
javascript                                                    Copy code

fetch('https://api.example.com/post-data', {
  method: 'POST',
  headers: {
    'Content-Type': 'application/json',
    // Add other headers as needed
  },
  body: JSON.stringify({ key1: 'value1', key2: 'value2' }),
})
  .then(response => response.json())
  .then(data => {
    // Handle the response
    console.log(data);
  })
  .catch(error => {
    // Handle errors
    console.error('Fetch error:', error);
  });
```

Handling JSON and Other Response Types

The Fetch API can handle a variety of response types, including JSON, text, Blob, and more. You can use methods like **.json()**, **.text()**, or **.blob()** to parse and process the response data according to your needs.

Cross-Origin Requests

The Fetch API also supports Cross-Origin Resource Sharing (CORS), allowing you to make requests to different domains while adhering to security restrictions. CORS headers on the server-side determine whether a resource can be accessed from a different origin.

Async/Await and Fetch

In modern JavaScript, you can further simplify Fetch operations using **async/await**. This allows you to write asynchronous code that looks almost synchronous,

making it more readable. Here's a Fetch example using
async/await:

```javascript
async function fetchData() {
  try {
    const response = await fetch('https://api.example.com/data');
    if (!response.ok) {
      throw new Error('Network response was not ok');
    }
    const data = await response.json();
    console.log(data);
  } catch (error) {
    console.error('Fetch error:', error);
  }
}
```

The Fetch API has revolutionized the way web developers interact with remote resources. Its simplicity, promise-based approach, and flexibility have made it a preferred choice for making HTTP requests in modern web applications. Whether you're fetching data from an API, posting form submissions, or interacting with remote services, the Fetch API empowers you to handle these tasks with ease and elegance.

As web development continues to evolve, the Fetch API remains a valuable tool for building efficient and responsive web applications.

Demystifying Authentication: Ensuring Digital Identity and Security

In today's digital landscape, where access to information and services is a keystroke away, ensuring the integrity of user identities and securing online interactions has never been more critical. Authentication serves as the gatekeeper, verifying the identity of users and granting access only to those who can provide valid credentials. In this exploration, we will delve into the realm of authentication, understanding its importance, methods, and the role it plays in safeguarding digital ecosystems.

What is Authentication?

Authentication is the process of confirming the identity of a user, device, or system entity attempting to access a protected resource or service. It answers the fundamental question: "Who are you?" The primary goal of authentication is to ensure that only authorized individuals or entities gain access while keeping unauthorized users at bay.

The Importance of Authentication

Authentication forms the foundation of digital security and trust. It is the first line of defense against unauthorized access, data breaches, and fraudulent activities. By confirming the identity of users or devices, authentication establishes a level of trust that enables secure interactions, protects sensitive information, and ensures compliance with privacy regulations.

Methods of Authentication

Authentication can take various forms, depending on the level of security required and the context of use. Here are some common methods:

1. **Password-based Authentication**: This is perhaps the most familiar form of authentication. Users provide a username and a secret password, which must match the stored credentials in a database. However, passwords are susceptible to breaches if not properly managed.

2. **Two-factor Authentication (2FA)**: 2FA adds an extra layer of security by requiring users to provide two separate authentication factors. These factors can include something the user knows (password), something the user has (a mobile device or smart card), or something the user is (biometric data like fingerprints or facial recognition).

3. **Multi-factor Authentication (MFA)**: MFA goes a step further by incorporating multiple authentication factors from different categories. For example, a user might need to provide a password, a fingerprint scan, and a time-based one-time password (TOTP).

4. **Biometric Authentication**: Biometric methods use unique physical or behavioral characteristics, such as fingerprints, facial features, or voice patterns, to confirm identity. Biometrics provide a high level of security and convenience.

5. **Token-based Authentication**: Tokens are physical or digital devices that generate time-sensitive codes. Users must enter the current code along with their password to gain access. Tokens are often used for remote access or secure transactions.

6. **Certificate-based Authentication**: In this method, users are issued digital certificates that contain a public key. Authentication relies on the user's possession of the private key corresponding to the certificate's public key.

7. **Single Sign-On (SSO)**: SSO allows users to log in once and access multiple services or applications without repeatedly entering credentials. It streamlines user experience while maintaining security.

Security Challenges and Best Practices

While authentication is crucial, it is not without its challenges. Passwords can be weak or easily compromised, and even strong passwords can be stolen. To enhance security, best practices include:

- Encouraging the use of strong, unique passwords.

- Regularly updating passwords.

- Implementing password policies, such as complexity requirements and expiration periods.

- Enforcing account lockout after multiple failed login attempts.

- Monitoring and logging authentication events for anomaly detection

Handling Data and User Input

Handling data and user input is a critical aspect of Chrome extension development, pivotal in creating a seamless and secure user experience.

Local Storage provides a means to store small amounts of user-specific data on the client's device, enabling the persistence of settings and preferences across sessions. Sync Storage takes it a step further, allowing data synchronization across multiple devices for users logged into Chrome, enhancing accessibility and convenience.

Data Validation ensures the integrity and security of data, safeguarding against vulnerabilities originating from external sources or user inputs. Robust validation and sanitization techniques are essential for preventing common security threats like cross-site scripting (XSS) attacks.

Effective User Input Handling includes strategies for managing form submissions, responding to user interactions, and applying validation procedures. By implementing best practices in data management and input handling, Chrome extensions can offer users a reliable and secure environment while delivering the desired functionality.

Local Storage: Local Storage is a vital tool for managing small amounts of data on the user's device. It allows your extension to store preferences, settings, and other essential information locally. This means that even if the user closes their browser or reboots their computer, your extension can retrieve their preferences and provide a consistent experience.

Sync Storage: Sync Storage takes data management a step further by enabling synchronization across multiple devices for users logged into Chrome. This feature is especially valuable for extensions that aim to offer a consistent experience across various platforms. You'll learn how to implement sync storage effectively, ensuring that users have access to their data wherever they use your extension.

Data Validation: Security is paramount in extension development. When dealing with data from external sources or user inputs, data validation is critical. Learn how to validate and sanitize data to prevent security vulnerabilities. By doing so, you protect your extension and its users from potential threats like cross-site scripting (XSS) attacks and injection vulnerabilities.

User Input Handling: Handling user input is a fundamental aspect of extension development. This includes managing form submissions, responding to user interactions, and applying data validation techniques. You'll discover best practices for making your extension user-friendly and secure.

Organizing Code for Enhanced Functionality: Best Practices in Software Architecture

In the realm of software development, code organization stands as the foundation upon which robust and maintainable applications are built. Effective organization not only streamlines development but also enhances functionality, readability, and long-term scalability. In this comprehensive exploration, we delve into the significance of code organization, its challenges, and best practices that lead to better functionality.

Best Practices in Code Organization

To excel in code organization and achieve better functionality, developers should adhere to best practices:

1. **Modularization:** Divide code into modules or components, each responsible for a specific functionality or feature. This promotes encapsulation and allows for easy unit testing.

2. **Clear Naming Conventions:** Adopt clear and consistent naming conventions for variables, functions, classes, and modules. This enhances code readability and maintainability.

3. **Separation of Concerns:** Follow the principle of "separation of concerns," which advocates keeping different aspects of the application (e.g., data access, business logic, user interface) in separate modules or layers.

4. **Use of Design Patterns:** Utilize design patterns, such as the Model-View-Controller (MVC) or Model-View-ViewModel (MVVM), to guide the organization of code in applications. These patterns provide a structured approach to code architecture.

5. **Comments and Documentation:** Include comments and documentation that explain the purpose and usage of functions, classes, and modules. This aids developers in understanding and maintaining the code.

6. **Version Control:** Implement version control systems like Git to track changes, collaborate effectively, and roll back to previous code states when necessary.

7. **Testing:** Develop unit tests for individual modules to ensure that they function as intended. This verifies that changes or updates do not introduce unintended side effects.

Modularization: Unlocking Scalability and Maintainability in Software

In the world of software development, modularization stands as a pivotal concept that empowers developers to create scalable, maintainable, and efficient applications. It's the practice of breaking down a software system into smaller, self-contained modules, each responsible for a specific function or feature. In this exploration, we delve into the significance of modularization, its advantages, and best practices for harnessing its potential.

Best Practices in Modularization

To maximize the benefits of modularization and achieve scalable and maintainable software, developers should follow best practices:

1. **Clear Module Boundaries:** Define clear and logical boundaries for modules, ensuring that each module has a single, well-defined responsibility.

2. **Encapsulation:** Encapsulate data and functionality within modules, exposing only what's necessary for other modules to interact with.

3. **Dependency Management:** Manage dependencies between modules carefully. Avoid excessive coupling, where one module depends heavily on another.

4. **Testing:** Develop unit tests for individual modules to ensure that they function correctly and to catch issues early in the development process.

5. **Documentation:** Provide documentation for module interfaces, explaining how they should be used and any constraints or requirements.

6. **Version Control:** Utilize version control systems to track changes to modules, enabling collaboration and rollbacks when necessary.

Background Scripts: The Silent Workers of Your Chrome Extension

In the world of Chrome extensions, background scripts play a crucial behind-the-scenes role, managing tasks that need continuous execution, data storage, and communication between extension components. They are the silent workers ensuring your extension functions seamlessly while users interact with the browser. In this exploration, we delve into the significance of background scripts, their responsibilities, and best practices for effective implementation.

The Significance of Background Scripts

Imagine you're using a Chrome extension that tracks your online activity to provide customized recommendations. While you browse the web, this extension continuously collects data, processes it, and updates its recommendations in real-time. This continuous background operation is made possible by background scripts.

1. **Continuous Execution:** Background scripts run continuously in the background, even when the extension's popup or content scripts are not active. They can perform tasks like data collection, updates, and notifications without interrupting the user's browsing experience.

2. **Data Storage:** Background scripts are responsible for managing extension data. They can store and retrieve data, making it accessible to other extension components.

3. **Event Handling:** They can listen for specific events or triggers, such as user interactions or changes in browser state, and respond accordingly. For instance, a background script can monitor tabs and perform actions when specific URLs are opened.

4. **Communication Hub:** Background scripts act as a communication hub, facilitating interaction between different parts of the extension. They can send and receive messages to and from popup scripts, content scripts, and other background scripts.

Challenges in Background Scripts

While background scripts offer numerous advantages, they also present some challenges:

1. **Resource Usage:** Background scripts run continuously, consuming system resources. Poorly optimized scripts can impact browser performance.

2. **Complexity:** Managing and coordinating tasks in background scripts can become complex as the extension's functionality grows.

3. **Data Sharing:** Ensuring secure and efficient data sharing between background scripts and other extension components requires careful design.

Best Practices in Background Scripts

To maximize the benefits of background scripts and ensure they perform their role effectively, developers should follow best practices:

1. **Optimization:** Write efficient code to minimize resource usage. Avoid memory leaks and excessive CPU consumption.

2. **Event Handling:** Use event-driven programming to respond to events and triggers effectively. Prioritize events that are critical to the extension's functionality.

3. **Data Storage:** Choose appropriate storage mechanisms for extension data. Use local storage or sync storage for data persistence, and consider memory caching for frequently accessed data.

4. **Messaging:** Use the messaging system provided by the Chrome extension API to enable communication between background scripts and other extension components. Follow a clear message protocol.

5. **Security:** Be mindful of security. Sanitize and validate data coming from external sources to prevent security vulnerabilities.

6. **Testing:** Develop unit tests for critical functionality in background scripts to ensure they work correctly and handle edge cases.

7. **Documentation:** Document the purpose and responsibilities of each background script and the events they listen to. Clear documentation aids in maintenance and collaboration.

Writing a background script for a Chrome extension can be a complex undertaking.

If you're eager to delve deeper into the intricacies of background scripts and master their development, we invite you to explore our dedicated book on the subject:

"Background Scripts for Chrome Extensions." This comprehensive guide provides in-depth insights, practical examples, and advanced techniques for harnessing the full potential of background scripts. Whether you're a novice or an experienced developer, this resource will equip you with the knowledge and skills needed to create robust and efficient background scripts to complement your Chrome extensions.

Seamless Integration: The Power of Content Scripts in Your Chrome Extension

Content scripts are the bridge that connects your Chrome extension to the web pages users visit. They enable dynamic interactions, data manipulation, and injection of custom functionality into web content. In this exploration, we dive into the significance of content scripts, their role in enhancing user experiences, and best practices for seamless integration.

The Significance of Content Scripts

Picture a Chrome extension that enhances your social media experience by adding interactive buttons to posts, making your interactions more efficient. Content scripts make this possible by injecting custom code into web pages, allowing your extension to interact with web content.

1. **Dynamic Enhancements:** Content scripts enable real-time enhancements to web pages. They can modify the DOM (Document Object Model), add elements, or alter existing content, providing users with a richer browsing experience.

2. **Interaction:** Content scripts can listen for user interactions on web pages and trigger actions in

response. For instance, they can detect when a user clicks a button or hovers over an element and execute predefined actions.

3. **Data Extraction:** They facilitate data extraction from web pages, enabling your extension to gather information, parse content, or even scrape data for specific purposes.

4. **Customization:** Content scripts allow users to customize their web experience by injecting custom styles, scripts, or elements tailored to their preferences.

Challenges in Content Script Integration

While content scripts offer powerful capabilities, they come with certain challenges:

1. **Isolation:** Content scripts operate in an isolated environment, separate from the extension's background scripts. Coordinating communication and data sharing can be complex.

2. **DOM Changes:** Manipulating the DOM of web pages must be done carefully to avoid conflicts with existing page elements or scripts.

3. **Performance Impact:** Poorly optimized content scripts can impact page loading times and responsiveness.

Best Practices in Content Script Integration

To harness the full potential of content scripts and ensure seamless integration, developers should follow best practices:

1. **Isolation and Messaging:** Use the messaging system provided by the Chrome extension API to facilitate communication between content scripts and background scripts. Clearly define message protocols for effective data exchange.

2. **Selective Injection:** Specify the URLs where content scripts should run to avoid unnecessary resource consumption. Define patterns in the manifest file that determine when content scripts are injected.

3. **DOM Manipulation:** Be cautious when manipulating the DOM to prevent conflicts with existing page elements. Use appropriate JavaScript libraries to simplify DOM interactions.

4. **Event Handling:** Employ event-driven programming to respond to user interactions and page changes effectively. Prioritize event listeners that are essential to the extension's functionality.

5. **Performance Optimization:** Write efficient code to minimize resource usage. Avoid excessive CPU or memory consumption in content scripts.

6. **Testing:** Develop unit tests to ensure content scripts work correctly and handle various scenarios, including different web page structures.

Crafting a content script for a Chrome extension can be a complex endeavour:

If you're eager to unravel the intricacies of content scripts and become proficient in their development, we recommend exploring our dedicated book:

*, **"Content Scripts for Chrome Extensions."** This comprehensive resource offers in-depth guidance, practical examples, and advanced strategies for mastering content script creation. Whether you're a beginner or an experienced developer, this book will empower you with the knowledge and skills necessary to craft efficient and effective content scripts, enriching your Chrome extensions with dynamic interactions and seamless integration with web pages.*

Chapter 7: Storing Data in Chrome Extensions

Introduction

Understanding the Significance of Data Storage in Chrome Extensions

In the realm of Chrome extensions, data storage serves as the backbone, allowing these innovative plugins to fulfill their intended purposes seamlessly. The significance of data storage becomes apparent when we consider its pivotal roles:

Remembering User Preferences

Chrome extensions are all about customization and user experience. Users appreciate having the ability to tailor the extension to their unique needs and preferences. Imagine having to reset your preferences every time you open your browser or reload an extension – it would be an inconvenient and frustrating experience. Effective data storage in Chrome extensions allows users to customize their settings once, and these choices persist across sessions. This not only enhances user satisfaction but also simplifies their interactions with the extension, making it more user-friendly and intuitive.

Enhancing Performance

In the fast-paced digital world, every second counts. Users demand speed and efficiency in their web experiences. Chrome extensions often rely on external data sources or APIs to provide real-time information or updates. However, making repeated network requests can introduce significant latency, resulting in a sluggish user experience. Data storage solutions come to the rescue by allowing extensions to cache frequently accessed data locally. This means that instead of fetching the same data repeatedly from the internet, the extension can quickly retrieve it from local storage. This not only speeds up the extension's performance but also reduces the load on external servers, contributing to a smoother and more efficient browsing experience.

Supporting Offline Usage

The internet is not always accessible. Users may find themselves in situations where they have limited or no internet connectivity. In such cases, Chrome extensions equipped with effective data storage mechanisms can continue functioning seamlessly. By storing essential data locally, these extensions can operate even when the user's device is offline, ensuring uninterrupted access to critical features. This offline support not only enhances the extension's reliability but also adds to its overall utility, making it a dependable tool regardless of the user's internet connection status.

1. Local Storage: Empowering Your Chrome Extension

Tagline: Where Simplicity Meets Persistence

Local Storage, a cornerstone of data management in Chrome extensions, embodies simplicity and resilience. This lightweight storage mechanism allows you to store key-value pairs directly within the user's browser, offering seamless data access and preservation even after the browser is closed.

The Essence of Local Storage

Local Storage is designed for the uncomplicated yet essential task of data retention. It provides Chrome extensions with a straightforward and persistent storage solution. Here's why Local Storage stands out:

Simplicity in Design: Local Storage operates on the principle of simplicity. It offers an intuitive approach to storing data, with key-value pairs that can be easily set, retrieved, and updated through JavaScript. This straightforward design ensures that even developers new to Chrome extensions can quickly grasp its usage.

Browser-Level Persistence: What sets Local Storage apart is its ability to endure. When data is stored using this mechanism, it remains intact and accessible even after the user closes their browser. This means that user preferences, customizations, and critical information can be conveniently retained between browsing sessions.

User-Centric Approach: Chrome extensions thrive on enhancing user experiences, and Local Storage plays a pivotal role in achieving this. By allowing users to tailor their extension settings and preferences, it contributes to a more personalized and user-centric interaction.

Effortless Data Access: Retrieving data from Local Storage is effortless. With just a few lines of code, extensions can access the stored information, making it ideal for quick and frequent data operations.

Use Cases for Local Storage

Local Storage's simplicity and persistence make it a versatile choice for various use cases in Chrome extensions:

User Preferences: Store user preferences, settings, and customizations to maintain a consistent user experience.

Session Management: Manage session-specific data, such as login tokens or temporary states, conveniently.

Quick Data Access: Utilize Local Storage for frequently accessed data, reducing the need for repeated network requests and enhancing performance.

Customization: Empower users to personalize their extension by storing layout preferences, theme choices, or saved content.

In essence, Local Storage is your extension's dependable companion, providing a straightforward and resilient means to store and retrieve essential data. Whether it's enhancing user experiences, improving performance, or simply remembering user choices, Local Storage simplifies data management, ensuring your Chrome extension is both user-friendly and efficient.

2. Sync Storage: Unifying User Experiences Across Devices

Tagline: Bridging Devices, Empowering Consistency

In the dynamic landscape of Chrome extensions, ensuring a seamless user experience across multiple devices is paramount. This is where Sync Storage steps in as a crucial data storage mechanism, facilitating the synchronization of user data when they are logged into Chrome. With its tagline, "Bridging Devices, Empowering Consistency," Sync Storage encapsulates its essence and importance.

The Power of Sync Storage

Sync Storage is the backbone for extensions that aim to provide users with a unified experience, no matter which device they are using. Here's why Sync Storage is indispensable:

Cross-Device Synchronization: Sync Storage excels in harmonizing user data between devices. When a user logs into Chrome, their extension's data, preferences, and settings seamlessly propagate across all devices. This ensures that users encounter a consistent extension experience, regardless of where they access it.

User-Centric Data Handling: Chrome extensions thrive on enhancing user convenience, and Sync Storage aligns perfectly with this objective. By enabling the preservation and synchronization of user-centric data, such as preferences, bookmarks, and history, it empowers users to have a uniform experience across their digital ecosystem.

Data Resilience: Sync Storage ensures that user data remains resilient and secure. Even if a device is lost or replaced, the extension's data is readily available upon login, sparing users from the hassle of manual data migration or reconfiguration.

Efficiency and Performance: Extensions that rely on Sync Storage can enhance their efficiency. By centralizing data storage and management, they reduce redundant data entry and minimize the risk of inconsistencies between devices. This optimization leads to improved extension performance.

Use Cases for Sync Storage

Sync Storage's unique capabilities open up a plethora of use cases for Chrome extensions:

Cross-Platform Consistency: Maintain consistent extension settings, themes, and customizations across various devices, creating a unified user experience.

Bookmark and History Sync: Synchronize bookmarks, browsing history, and saved content, ensuring users can access their favorite resources from any device.

User Account Data: Store user account details, login credentials, and account-related settings securely, simplifying user access to online services.

Extension State Preservation: Preserve the state of the extension, including open tabs, active sessions, and recently viewed content, for uninterrupted browsing experiences.

Backup and Restore: Offer users the ability to back up their extension data to the cloud and restore it effortlessly on a new device.

Sync Storage emerges as a vital tool in the arsenal of Chrome extensions, promoting consistency, security, and user-centric data management. By embracing Sync Storage, extensions can bridge the gap between devices, ensuring that users enjoy a uniform, hassle-free experience throughout their digital journey.

3. Chrome Storage API: Your Gateway to Robust Data Management

Tagline: Elevate Your Extension with Intelligent Data Handling

In the realm of Chrome extensions, efficient data management is akin to the lifeblood that powers their functionality and enhances the user experience. The Chrome Storage API, often referred to as the secret ingredient behind many successful extensions, offers developers a versatile and robust means of handling data. With its tagline, "Elevate Your Extension with Intelligent Data Handling," the Chrome Storage API underscores its significance in creating feature-rich and responsive extensions.

The Versatility of Chrome Storage API

The Chrome Storage API stands out as a versatile solution, offering both local and sync storage options, providing developers with the flexibility needed to manage data effectively. Here's why this API is a game-changer:

1. Local and Sync Storage: One of the core strengths of the Chrome Storage API is its dual functionality. It provides developers with the option to choose between local and sync storage, depending on the specific needs of their extension.

- *Local Storage*: Developers can utilize local storage to store data directly on the user's device, ensuring quick access and low-latency retrieval. This is ideal for information that doesn't need to be synchronized across multiple devices but should persist across sessions.

- *Sync Storage*: Sync storage, on the other hand, enables seamless synchronization of data across devices for users logged into Chrome. This is particularly valuable for extensions that aim to provide a consistent user experience across various platforms.

2. Scalable Data Handling: The Chrome Storage API empowers developers to manage data efficiently, whether it's a small set of user preferences or a vast cache of information. Its scalability ensures that extensions can adapt to different data requirements without sacrificing performance.

3. Security and Privacy: Data security and user privacy are paramount in extension development. The API ensures that user data is stored securely, safeguarding it against unauthorized access or breaches.

Use Cases for Chrome Storage API

The Chrome Storage API unlocks a multitude of use cases, making it indispensable for a wide range of extensions:

1. **Customization and Preferences**: Extensions can utilize local storage to remember user preferences, such as

theme choices, layout configurations, or feature settings, ensuring a personalized browsing experience.

2. **Offline Content**: Developers can store cached content locally, enabling extensions to continue functioning seamlessly even when the user is offline.

3. **Cross-Device Synchronization**: For extensions that prioritize consistent experiences across devices, sync storage ensures that user data, including bookmarks, history, and settings, is synchronized effortlessly.

4. **User Authentication**: Chrome Storage API allows for secure storage of user authentication tokens and credentials, streamlining access to online services.

5. **Analytics and Usage Tracking**: Extensions can store usage data locally, providing valuable insights into user behavior and interaction patterns.

Best Practices with Chrome Storage API

To maximize the benefits of the Chrome Storage API, developers should adhere to best practices:

1. **Data Validation**: Ensure that data stored in the API is validated and sanitized to prevent security vulnerabilities.

2. **Minimal Data Storage**: Only store essential data to minimize the extension's footprint and reduce the risk of data breaches.

3. **Consistent Data Handling**: Maintain consistency in data handling between local and sync storage, providing a cohesive user experience.

4. **Periodic Data Sync**: Implement strategies for periodic data synchronization to keep sync storage up to date and minimize potential data conflicts.

The Chrome Storage API serves as a cornerstone for extension development, offering the tools needed to create feature-rich, efficient, and user-friendly extensions. Its ability to handle data seamlessly, coupled with the option for synchronization, empowers developers to elevate their extensions to new heights of functionality and performance.

Obtaining the Chrome Storage API: Your Key to Enhanced Data Management

In the world of Chrome extension development, the Chrome Storage API is a pivotal tool for managing data efficiently and improving user experiences. To harness its capabilities, developers must follow a straightforward process to obtain and implement this essential API.

Step 1: Create Your Chrome Extension

Before diving into the intricacies of the Chrome Storage API, you need to have a Chrome extension project underway. This typically involves defining your extension's purpose, functionality, and architecture.

Step 2: Define Your Data Storage Needs

To effectively utilize the Chrome Storage API, it's crucial to identify your extension's data storage requirements. Consider the following:

- What type of data does your extension need to store?

- Do you require local storage, sync storage, or both?

- How will the stored data enhance your extension's functionality?

Having a clear understanding of your data needs is essential for making the right decisions when implementing the Chrome Storage API.

Step 3: Incorporate the API into Your Extension

The Chrome Storage API is readily available as part of the Chrome Extensions platform. To incorporate it into your extension, follow these steps:

1. **Manifest File**: Open your extension's manifest file (usually named **manifest.json** and ensure that you declare permissions for storage. This grants your extension access to storage-related functions.

```json
"permissions": [
  "storage"
],
```

2. **JavaScript Implementation**: Within your extension's JavaScript code, you can now access the Chrome Storage API. Use the **chrome.storage** object to interact with the API. Here's a basic example of how to set and retrieve data using local storage:

```javascript
// Set data in local storage
chrome.storage.local.set({ key: 'value' }, function () {
  console.log('Data saved to local storage');
});

// Retrieve data from local storage
chrome.storage.local.get(['key'], function (result) {
  console.log('Retrieved data:', result.key);
});
```

For sync storage, replace **chrome.storage.local** with **chrome.storage.sync**.

Step 4: Data Management and Best Practices

Now that you have integrated the Chrome Storage API into your extension, it's essential to follow best practices for data management:

- **Data Validation**: Ensure that data stored in the API is validated and sanitized to prevent security vulnerabilities.

- **Minimal Data Storage**: Only store essential data to minimize the extension's footprint and reduce the risk of data breaches.

- **Consistent Data Handling**: Maintain consistency in data handling between local and sync storage, providing a cohesive user experience.

- **Periodic Data Sync**: Implement strategies for periodic data synchronization to keep sync storage up to date and minimize potential data conflicts.

By following these steps and best practices, you can successfully obtain and implement the Chrome Storage API, unlocking the power of efficient data management for your Chrome extension.

5. Web Storage API: Empowering Chrome Extensions with Local Data Storage

In the world of web and Chrome extension development, the Web Storage API is a valuable resource for efficiently managing data on the user's browser. This versatile API offers two distinct storage mechanisms: **localStorage** and **sessionStorage**, each catering to specific use cases. Let's explore the capabilities and advantages of the Web Storage API and how it can empower your Chrome extension.

Understanding Web Storage

Web Storage is a client-side data storage solution, meaning it stores data locally on the user's device rather than on a server. It offers two storage options:

1. **localStorage**: This provides a simple key-value storage mechanism with no expiration date. Data stored in **localStorage** remains available even after the browser is closed and reopened. It's ideal for persisting user preferences, settings, and other long-term data.

2. **sessionStorage**: Unlike **localStorage**, data stored in **sessionStorage** has a limited lifespan. It remains accessible only during the current browsing session and is cleared when the user closes the tab or browser. This is useful for temporarily storing data needed for a single session.

Advantages of Web Storage

The Web Storage API offers several advantages for Chrome extensions:

1. **Ease of Use**: Implementing Web Storage is straightforward. You can quickly store and retrieve data using JavaScript.

2. **Data Persistence**: 'localStorage' ensures that data remains available across browser sessions, allowing users to pick up where they left off.

3. **Lightweight**: Web Storage is a lightweight solution, ideal for extensions that don't require complex server-side data storage.

4. **No Network Dependency**: Since data is stored locally, there's no reliance on network connectivity, enhancing the extension's offline usability.

5. **Performance Boost**: Caching data in Web Storage can significantly improve an extension's performance by reducing the need for repeated network requests.

6. **User-Friendly**: Users appreciate extensions that remember their preferences and settings, and Web Storage facilitates this feature seamlessly.

Implementing Web Storage

To utilize Web Storage in your Chrome extension, follow these basic steps:

1. **Check Browser Support**: Confirm that the browser you're targeting supports the Web Storage API, which is a widely supported feature in modern browsers, including Chrome.

2. **Access Web Storage**: In your extension's JavaScript code, you can access **localStorage** and **sessionStorage** like this:

```javascript
// Storing data in localStorage
localStorage.setItem('key', 'value');

// Retrieving data from localStorage
const data = localStorage.getItem('key');
```

3. **Data Manipulation**: You can store strings, numbers, or serialized JSON objects in Web Storage. Be cautious with the amount of data you store, as there are storage limits.

4. **Data Removal**: To remove data, use the **remove Item(key)** method. For example:

```javascript
// Remove data from localStorage
localStorage.removeItem('key');
```

To obtain and use the Web Storage API in your Chrome extension, follow these steps:

1. **Create or Open Your Chrome Extension Project**: Ensure you have a Chrome extension project set up and accessible in your development environment.

2. **Add a JavaScript File**: In your extension project, create or include a JavaScript file where you'll write the code to interact with the Web Storage API. This file should be part of your extension's assets.

3. **Access Web Storage**: In your JavaScript file, you can access Web Storage through two objects: **localStorage** and **sessionStorage**. Decide which one suits your needs based on whether you need persistent storage (**localStorage**) or session-specific storage (**sessionStorage**).

4. **Store Data**: To store data in Web Storage, use the **setItem(key, value)** method, where **key** is a string representing the name of the item, and **value** is the data you want to store. For example:

```javascript
// Storing data in localStorage
localStorage.setItem('username', 'JohnDoe');
```

5. **Retrieve Data**: To retrieve data from Web Storage, use the **getItem(key)** method, where **key** is the name of the item you want to retrieve. For example:

```javascript
// Retrieving data from localStorage
const username = localStorage.getItem('username');
```

6. **Update Data**: To update the value of an item, simply set it again using '**setItem**'. This will overwrite the existing value associated with that key.

7. **Remove Data**: To remove data from Web Storage, use the **removeItem(key)** method, where **key** is the name of the item you want to delete. For example:

```javascript
// Removing data from localStorage
localStorage.removeItem('username');
```

8. **Clear All Data**: To clear all data stored in either **localStorage** or **sessionStorage**, use the **clear()** method. Be cautious when using this, as it removes all items stored under that storage mechanism.

```javascript
// Clearing all data in localStorage
localStorage.clear();
```

9. **Check for Existing Data**: Before retrieving data, it's a good practice to check if the data exists to prevent errors. You can use conditional statements like **if (localStorage.getItem('key')) { /* do something */ }**.

10. **Handle Errors**: Be prepared to handle errors that may occur when accessing Web Storage, such as exceeding storage limits or dealing with invalid data.

11. **Test Your Extension**: Test your Chrome extension to ensure that data is being stored and retrieved as expected. Debug any issues that may arise during testing.

12. **Implement Data Validation**: Always validate and sanitize data before storing it in Web Storage to prevent security vulnerabilities.

13. **Include Permissions**: In your extension's manifest file (**manifest.json**), make sure to include the necessary permissions if your extension interacts with external websites that require cross-origin data access. For example, if you need to access a specific website's data, you may need to declare **"permissions"** in the manifest file.

Once you've implemented these steps, your Chrome extension should be able to effectively use the Web Storage API to store and manage data locally in the user's browser. Remember to follow best practices and consider the specific requirements of your extension when deciding whether to use **localStorage** or **sessionStorage**.

6. Indexed DB

IndexedDB (Indexed Database) is a powerful client-side storage technology that allows web applications, including Chrome extensions, to store and manage large amounts of structured data. It provides a robust and efficient way to work with data locally in the browser, making it a valuable choice for building offline-capable and data-intensive applications.

Key Features of IndexedDB:

1. **Structured Data**: IndexedDB stores data in a structured format, typically as objects. This makes it suitable for managing complex data models, such as those used in applications requiring relational or hierarchical data.

2. **Asynchronous**: IndexedDB operations are asynchronous, which means they don't block the main thread of the browser. This is crucial for ensuring a smooth user experience, especially when dealing with large datasets.

3. **Indexed**: IndexedDB allows you to create indexes on properties of your data, improving query performance. These indexes enable efficient data retrieval based on specific criteria.

4. **Transaction-Based**: All operations in IndexedDB occur within transactions. Transactions ensure data consistency and provide a way to group multiple operations into a single unit of work.

5. **Scalable**: IndexedDB can handle substantial amounts of data, making it suitable for applications with extensive storage requirements. It is particularly useful for offline applications that need to cache and synchronize data.

6. **Cross-Origin Support**: IndexedDB supports cross-origin data access, allowing your Chrome extension to interact with databases hosted on different origins. However, you must request the appropriate permissions in your extension's manifest file.

Using IndexedDB in Chrome Extensions:

To use IndexedDB in a Chrome extension, you need to follow these steps:

1. **Open a Database**: Begin by opening a connection to an IndexedDB database. You can specify the database's name and version during this step.

2. **Create Object Stores**: An object store is where you store your data. Think of it as a table in a traditional relational database. Define the structure of your object stores, including keys and indexes.

3. **Add Data**: To add data to an object store, create a transaction and use the **add()** or **put()** method. The data you store can be in the form of JavaScript objects.

4. **Retrieve Data**: Use transactions to retrieve data from object stores. You can query data using indexes or iterate through the entire store.

5. **Update and Delete Data**: Transactions also enable you to update or delete data in object stores using the **put()** and **delete()** methods.

6. **Handling Transactions**: Be mindful of handling transactions properly to ensure data consistency. Transactions can be read-only or read-write, depending on your needs.

7. **Handling Errors**: IndexedDB operations can fail for various reasons, such as exceeding storage limits or database version mismatches. Implement error handling to gracefully manage these situations.

8. **Upgrading Databases**: As your extension evolves, you may need to modify the database structure. Use the **upgradeneeded** event to handle database schema changes during version updates.

9. **Closing the Database**: Always close the database connection when you're done using it to free up resources and prevent potential issues.

Indexed DB in Real-World Scenarios:

IndexedDB is commonly used in Chrome extensions for scenarios like:

- **Offline Data Storage**: It enables applications to work offline by caching data locally and synchronizing with a remote server when an internet connection is available.

- **Local Caching**: IndexedDB is used to store assets like images, scripts, and HTML files, reducing load times for web applications.

- **Structured Data Storage**: For applications requiring complex data models or those dealing with large datasets, IndexedDB provides an efficient and organized storage solution.

In conclusion, IndexedDB is a versatile and efficient data storage option for Chrome extensions. It empowers developers to create offline-capable applications, manage large datasets, and store structured data in a structured manner. By understanding the principles and best practices of IndexedDB, you can leverage its capabilities to enhance the functionality and performance of your Chrome extension.

Chapter 8: Troubleshooting and Testing Chrome Extensions

Troubleshooting and testing are critical aspects of Chrome extension development. Ensuring that your extension works as expected, even under various conditions and scenarios, is essential to providing a reliable user experience. In this chapter, we'll explore the key concepts, strategies, and tools for troubleshooting and testing Chrome extensions effectively.

The Importance of Troubleshooting and Testing

Before we dive into the specifics of troubleshooting and testing, let's understand why these processes are crucial for Chrome extension development:

1. **Quality Assurance**: Ensures that your extension functions correctly, reducing the risk of bugs or unexpected behavior that could frustrate users.

2. **Compatibility**: Verifies that your extension works seamlessly across different versions of Chrome and other browsers (if applicable).

3. **User Satisfaction**: A well-tested extension leads to a better user experience, which can result in higher user satisfaction and more positive reviews.

4. **Security**: Helps identify and address potential security vulnerabilities that could be exploited by malicious actors.

5. **Optimization**: Identifies performance bottlenecks and areas where optimization can enhance the extension's speed and responsiveness.

Troubleshooting Chrome Extensions

Troubleshooting involves diagnosing and resolving issues or bugs in your Chrome extension. Here are some troubleshooting strategies and best practices:

1. **Logging**: Use the **console.log()** function to output diagnostic information to the browser's console. This can help you track the flow of your extension's code and identify errors.

2. **Debugging Tools**: Chrome provides powerful debugging tools. You can set breakpoints, inspect variables, and step through your code to identify issues. Use the Chrome DevTools for this purpose.

3. **Error Messages**: Pay close attention to error messages and stack traces. They often provide valuable clues about the location and nature of the problem.

4. **Testing Environments**: Test your extension in various environments, including different Chrome versions and operating systems, to ensure compatibility.

5. **User Feedback**: Act on user feedback and bug reports promptly. Users can often provide valuable insights into issues they encounter.

Types of Testing

Testing involves systematically evaluating your extension's functionality, performance, and security. Here are the primary types of testing for Chrome extensions:

1. **Unit Testing**: Focuses on testing individual components or functions in isolation. Use JavaScript testing frameworks like Jest or Mocha to write unit tests for your extension.

2. **Integration Testing**: Evaluates how different components of your extension work together. Ensure

that interactions between background scripts, content scripts, and other components are seamless.

3. **Functional Testing**: Tests the functionality of your extension as a whole. This type of testing simulates real user interactions to verify that the extension performs its intended tasks correctly.

4. **Regression Testing**: Ensures that new code changes do not introduce new bugs or break existing functionality. Automate regression testing to save time.

5. **Performance Testing**: Measures the speed, responsiveness, and resource usage of your extension. This is essential for optimizing its performance.

6. **Security Testing**: Identifies potential security vulnerabilities, such as cross-site scripting (XSS) or data leakage issues. Tools like OWASP ZAP can help with security testing.

Automated Testing Tools

To streamline the testing process, consider using automated testing tools and frameworks tailored for Chrome extensions:

1. **Jest**: A popular JavaScript testing framework that is highly customizable and suitable for unit testing.

2. **Selenium**: An automation testing framework that can simulate user interactions with your extension.

3. **Cypress**: A modern end-to-end testing framework that is well-suited for testing web applications and Chrome extensions.

4. **Jasmine**: A behavior-driven testing framework that works well for testing JavaScript applications.

Continuous Integration (CI) and Continuous Deployment (CD)

Integrating your testing process into a CI/CD pipeline can further enhance the reliability and quality of your extension. CI/CD systems automatically build, test, and deploy your extension whenever code changes are made, reducing the likelihood of introducing bugs and ensuring that users always receive the latest, stable version.

User Acceptance Testing (UAT)

Before releasing your extension to a wider audience, consider conducting User Acceptance Testing (UAT). This involves getting feedback from a group of users who represent your target audience. UAT helps identify usability issues, gather feedback on user experience, and ensure that your extension meets user expectations.

Conclusion

Troubleshooting and testing are indispensable aspects of Chrome extension development. By diligently identifying and addressing issues, thoroughly testing your extension, and leveraging automated testing tools, you can deliver a reliable, performant, and secure extension that enhances the browsing experience for your users. In the next sections of this chapter, we will dive deeper into specific testing techniques and tools to empower you to build and maintain high-quality Chrome extensions.

www.ingramcontent.com/pod-product-compliance
Lightning Source LLC
LaVergne TN
LVHW041214050326
832903LV00021B/613